# Dragons Coloring Book

## Dragons Coloring Book for Kids Activity Books for Kids

ISBN-13: 978-1982045265
ISBN-10: 1982045264

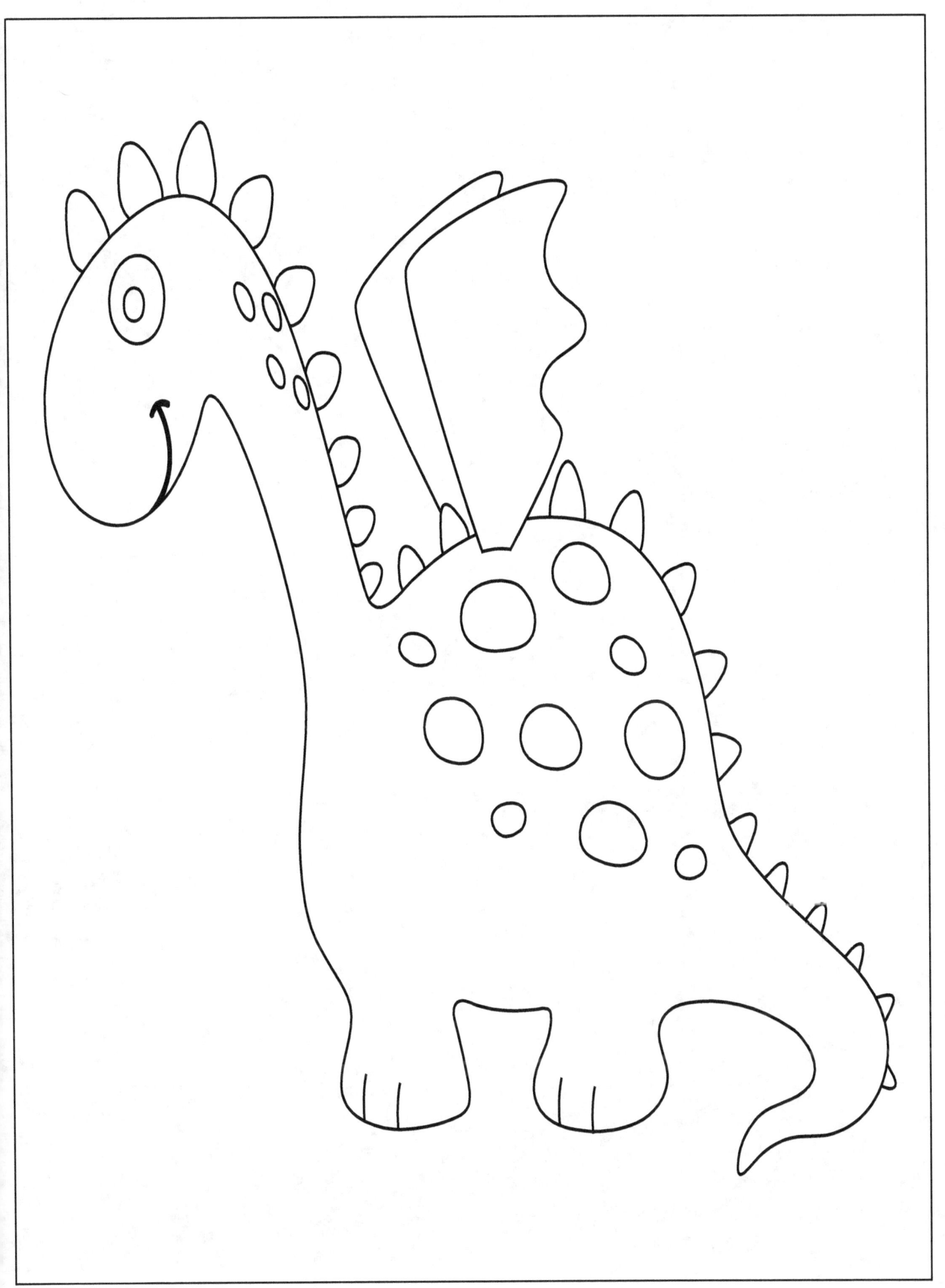

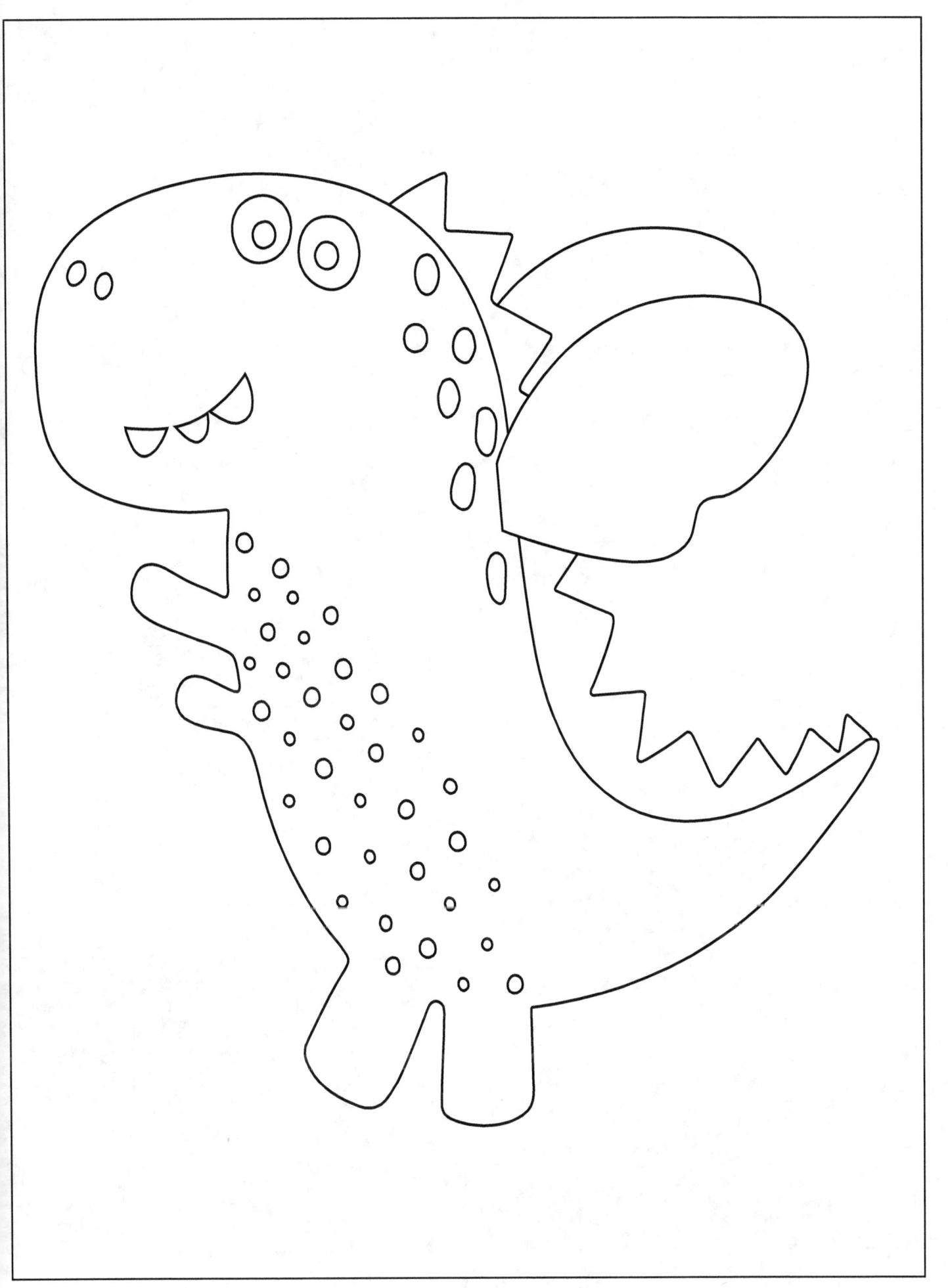

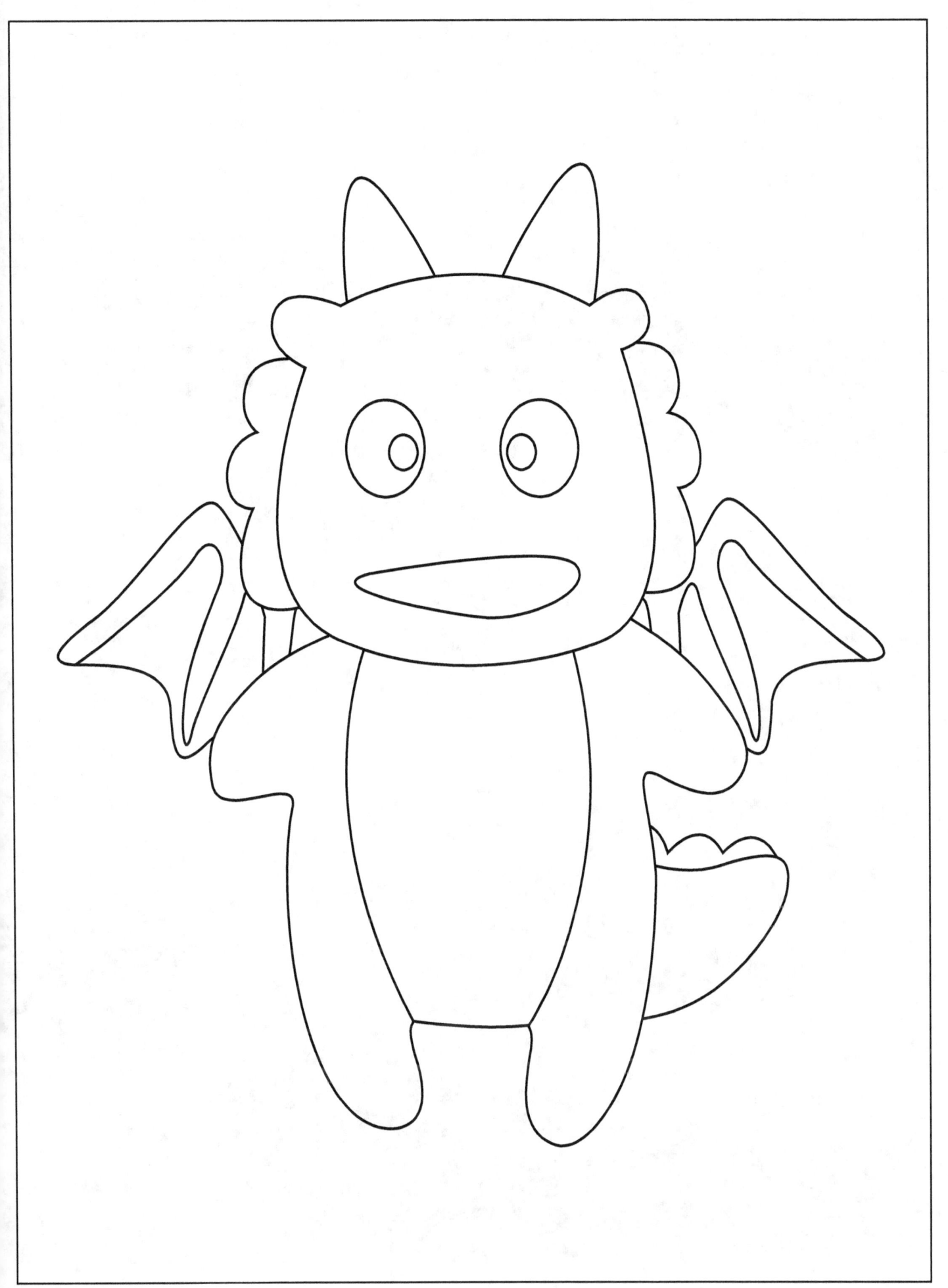

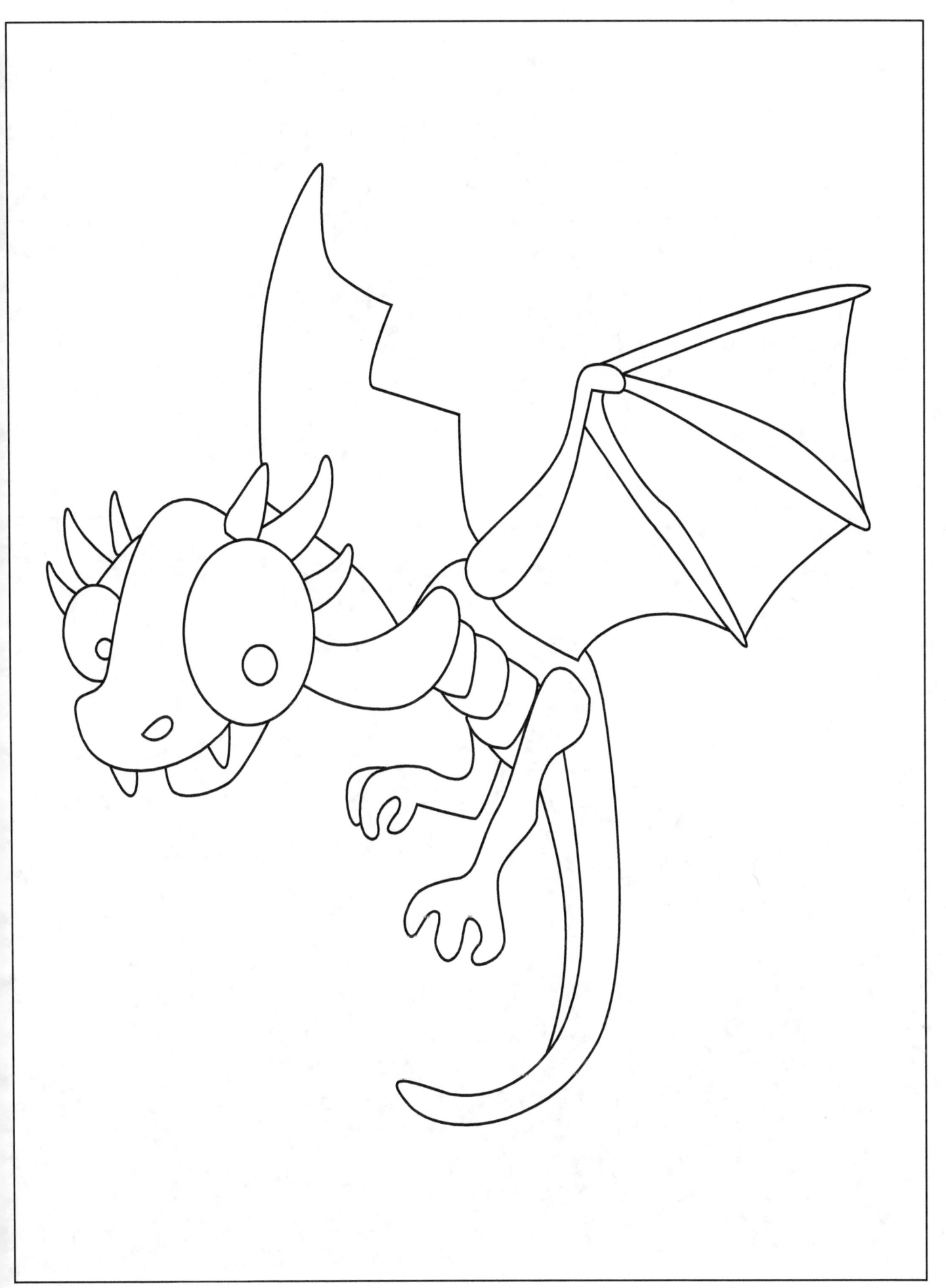

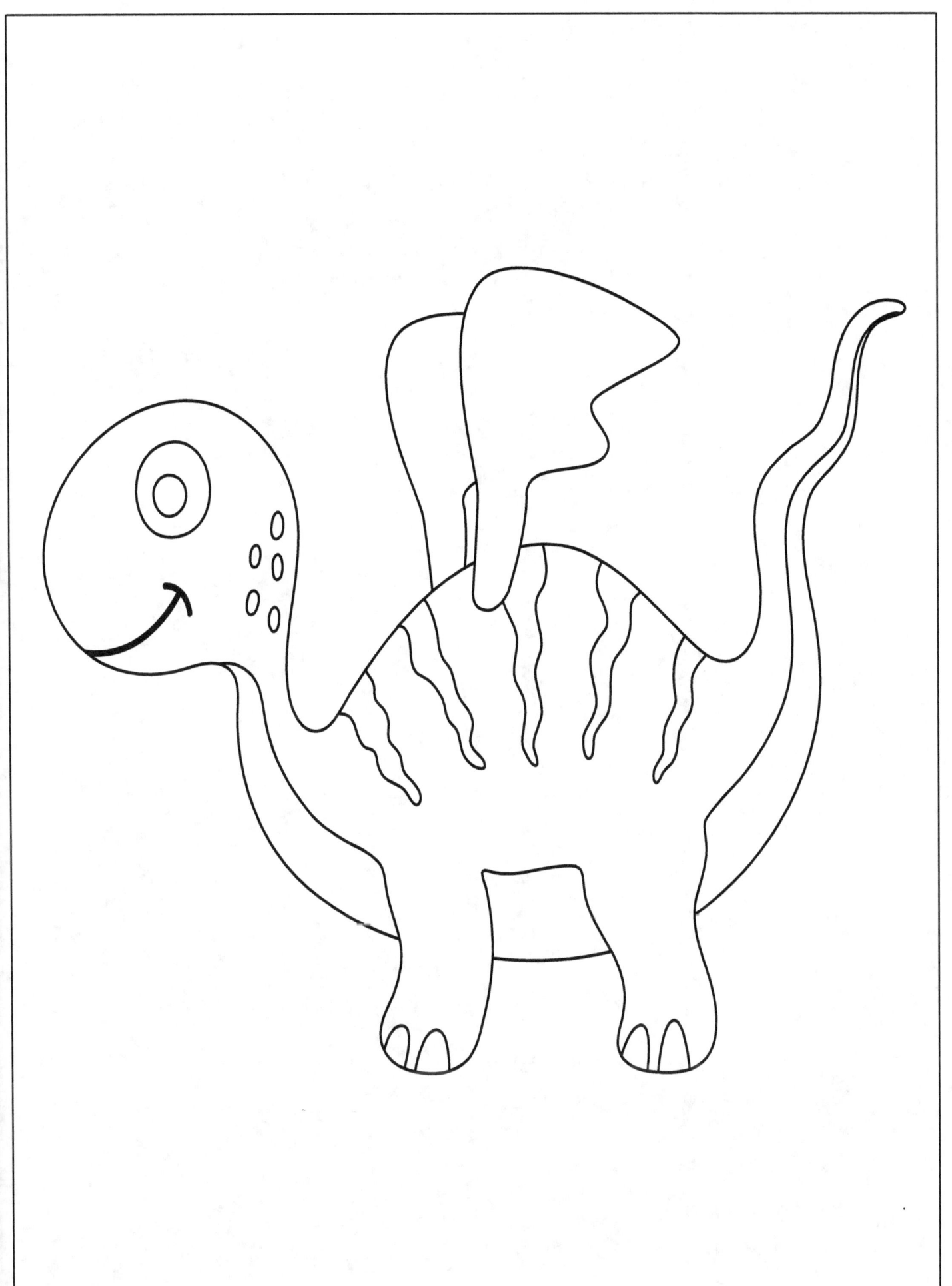

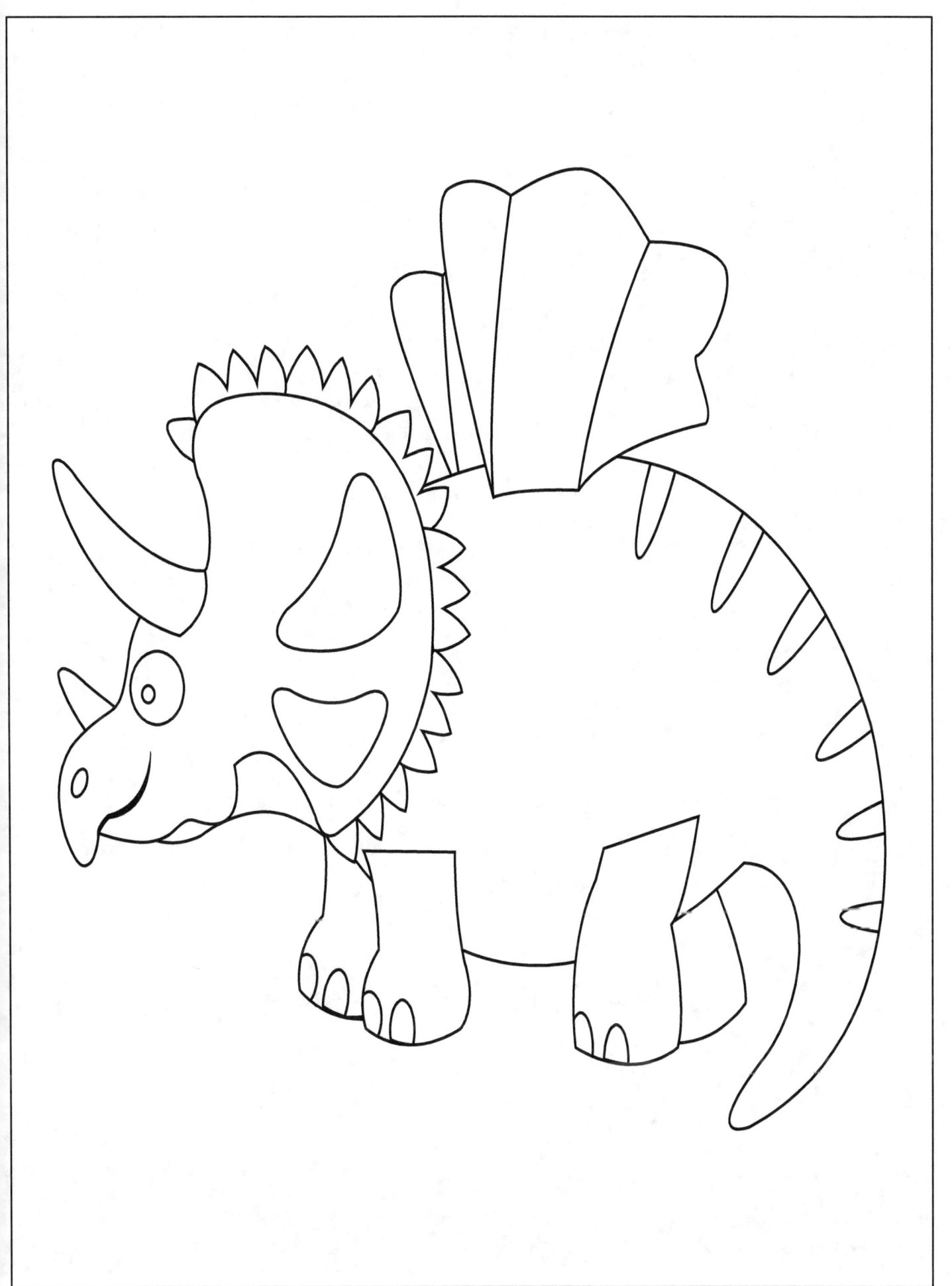

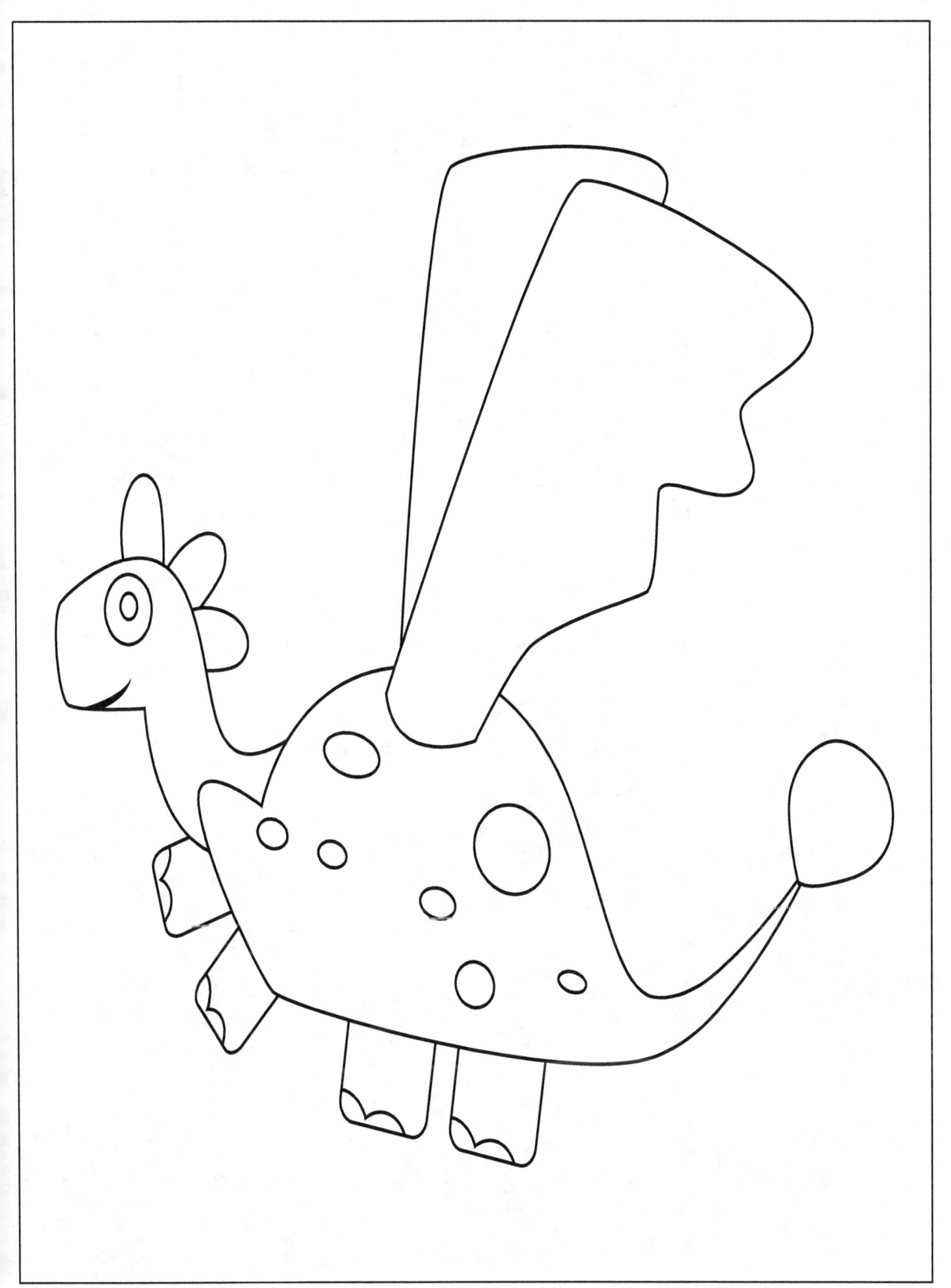

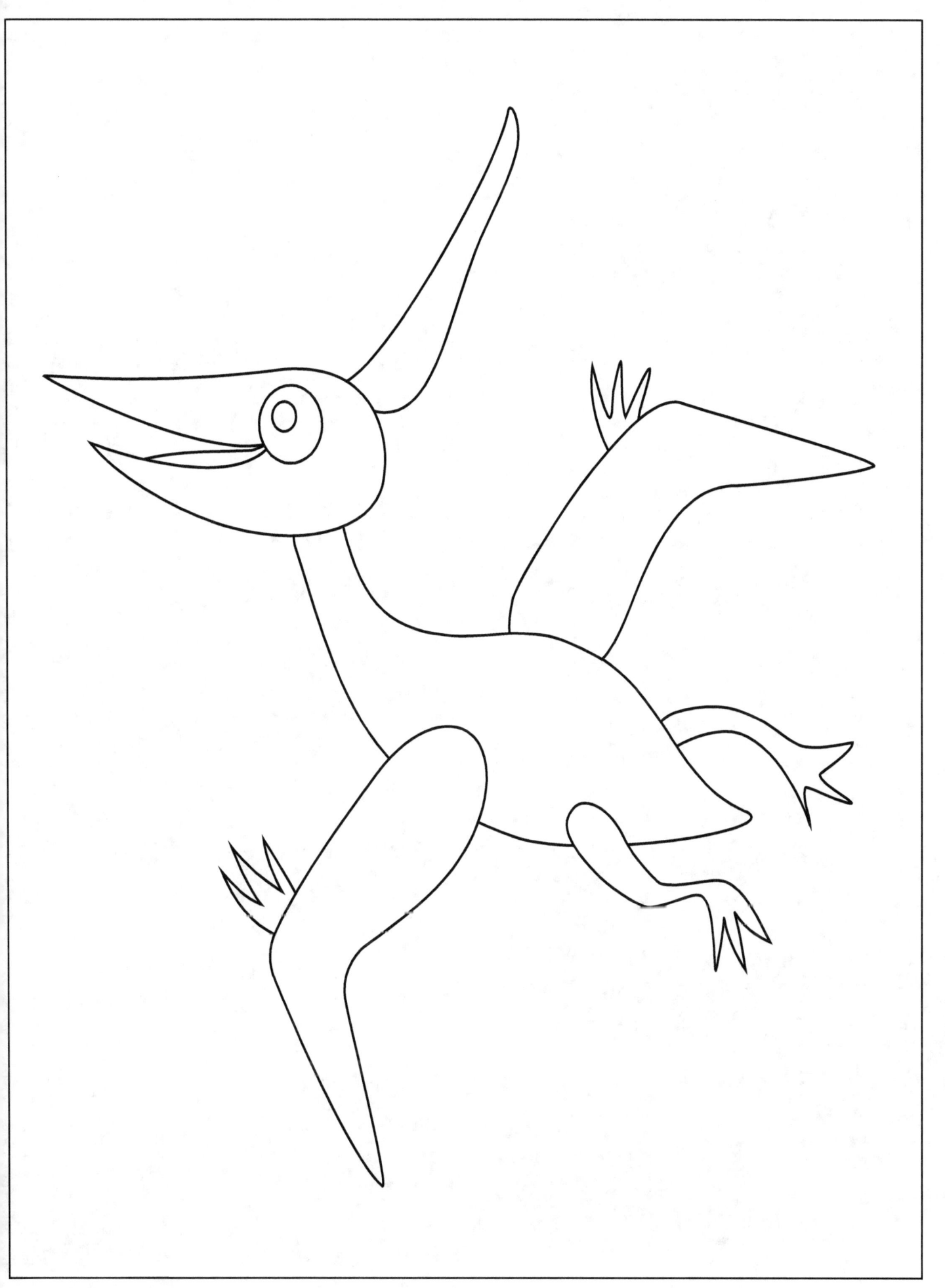

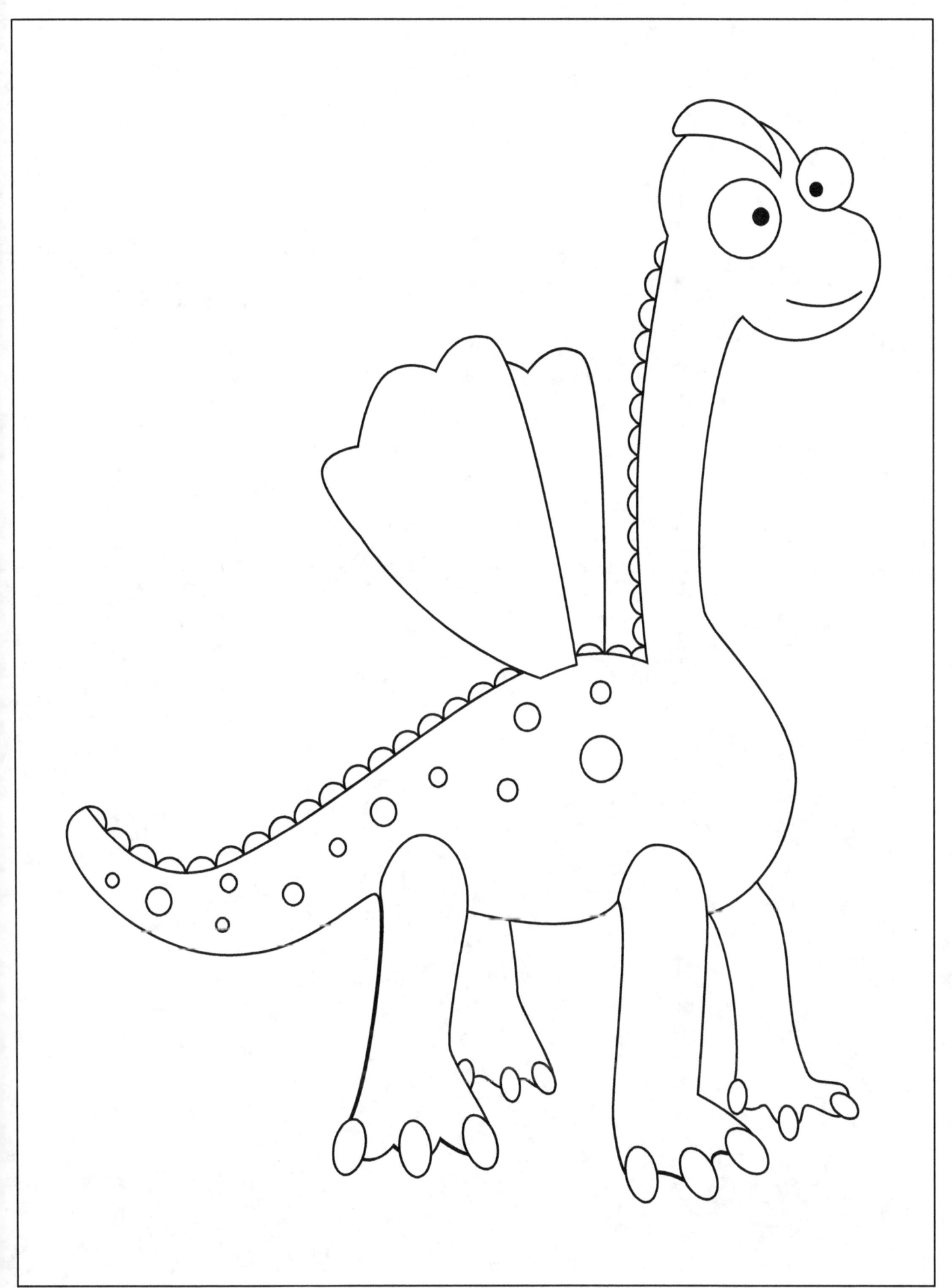

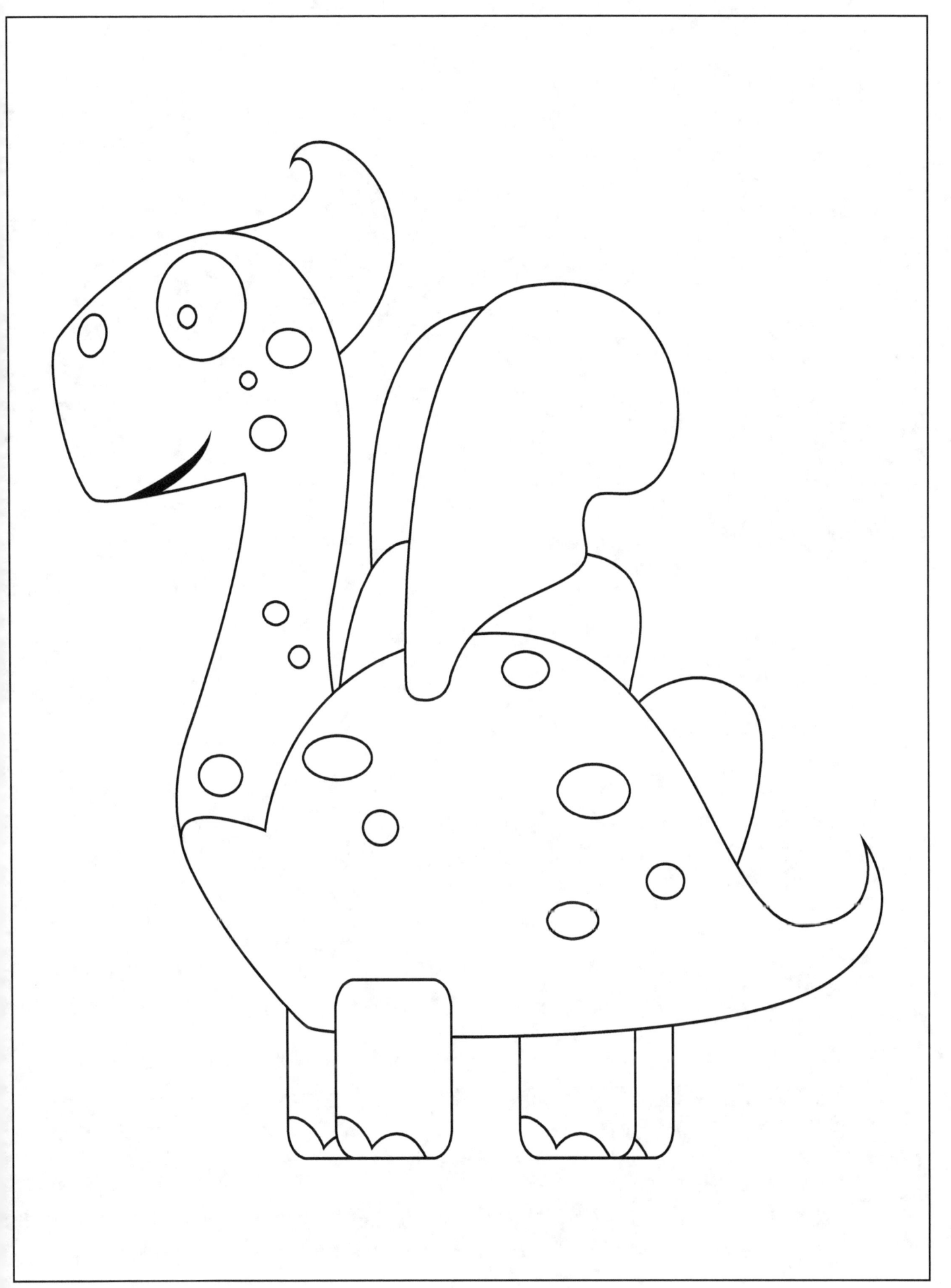

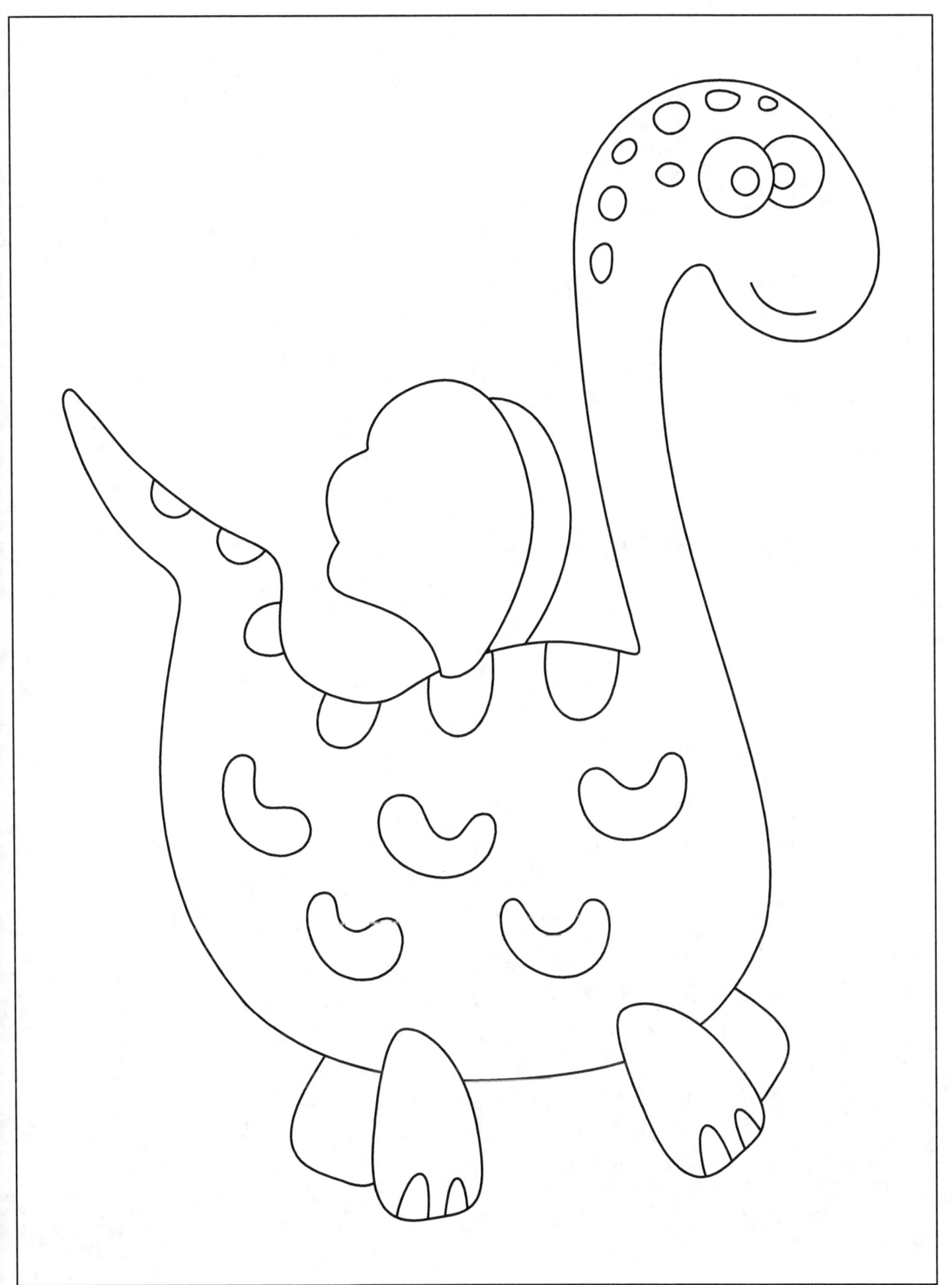

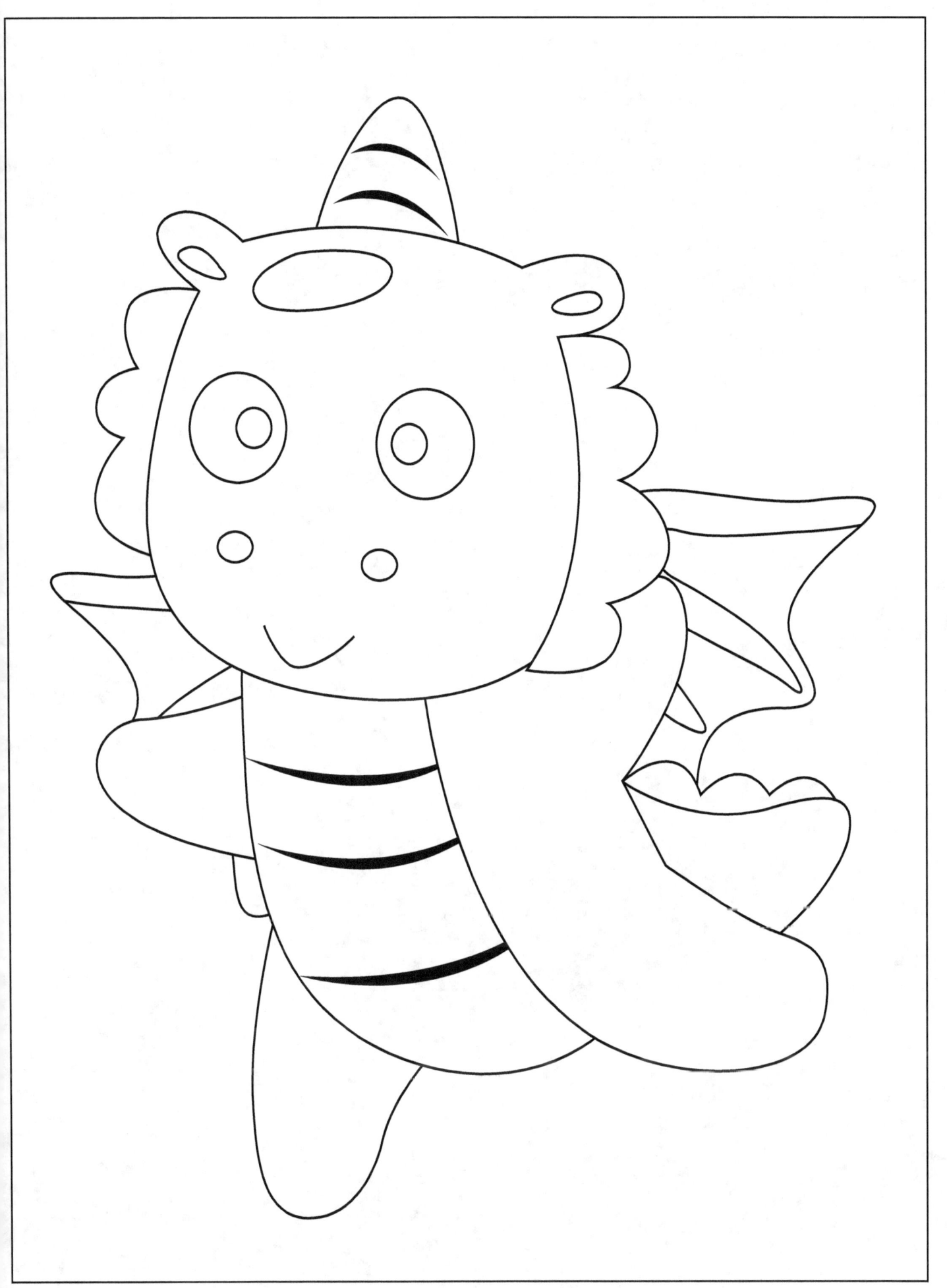

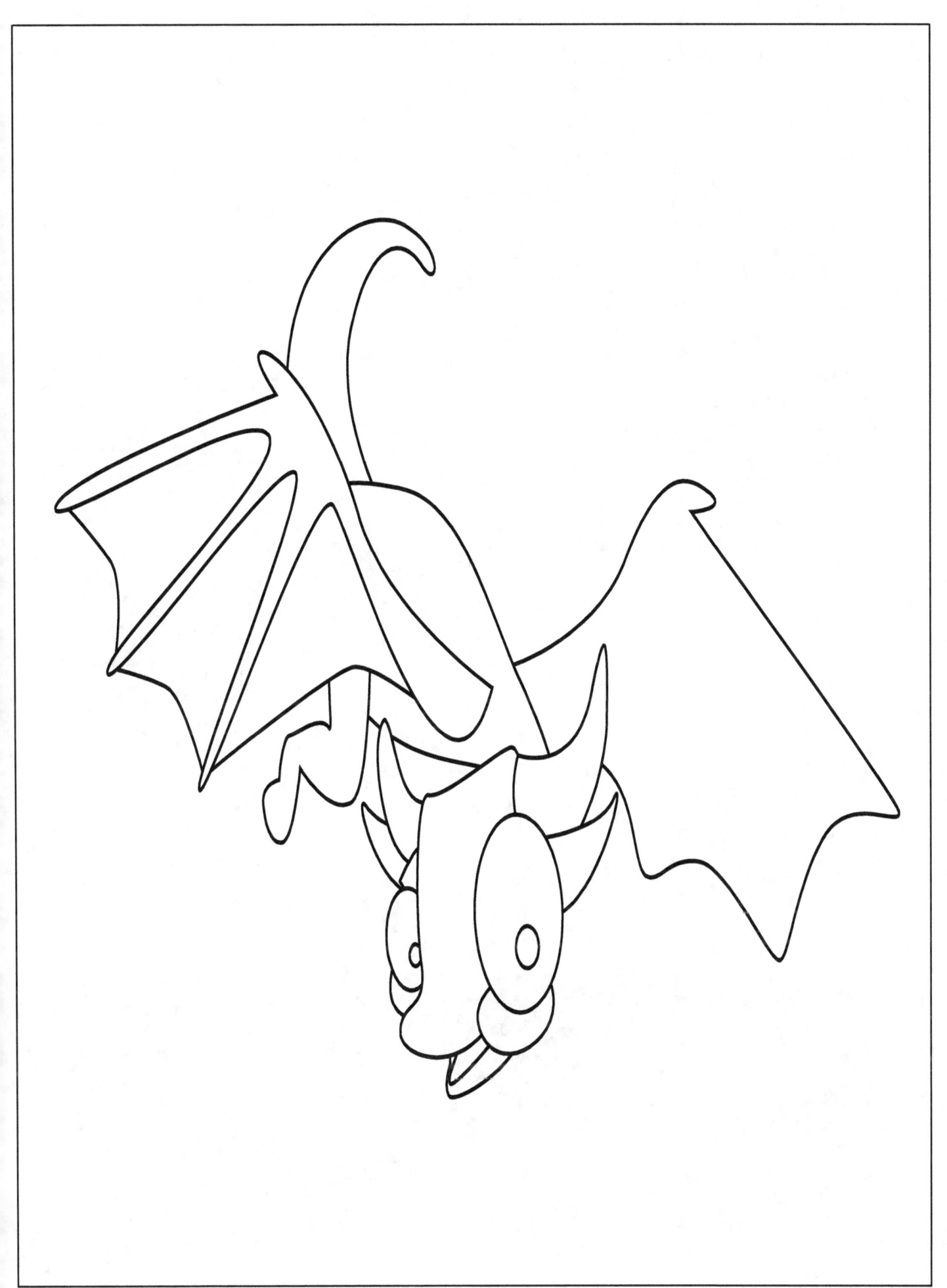

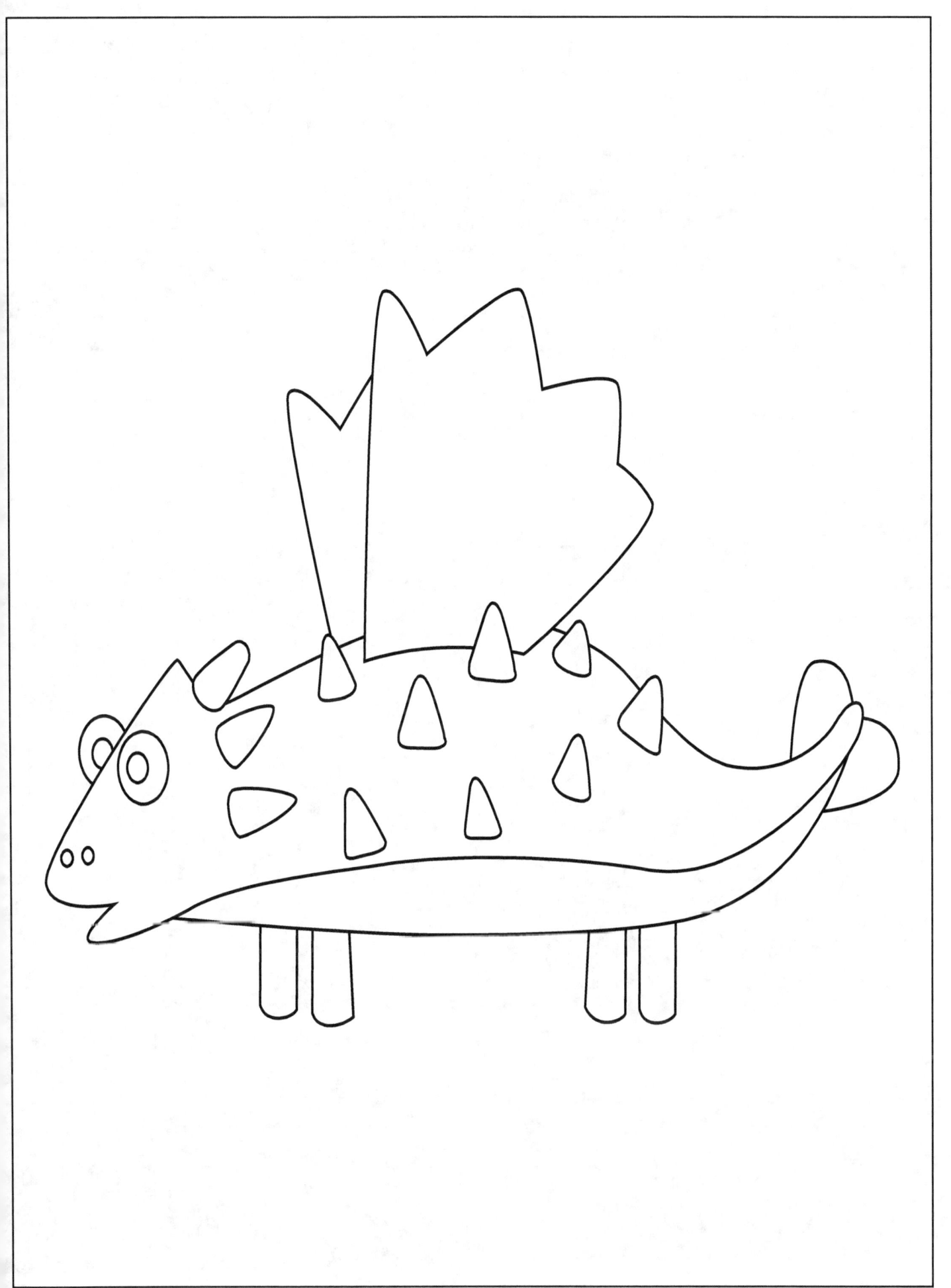

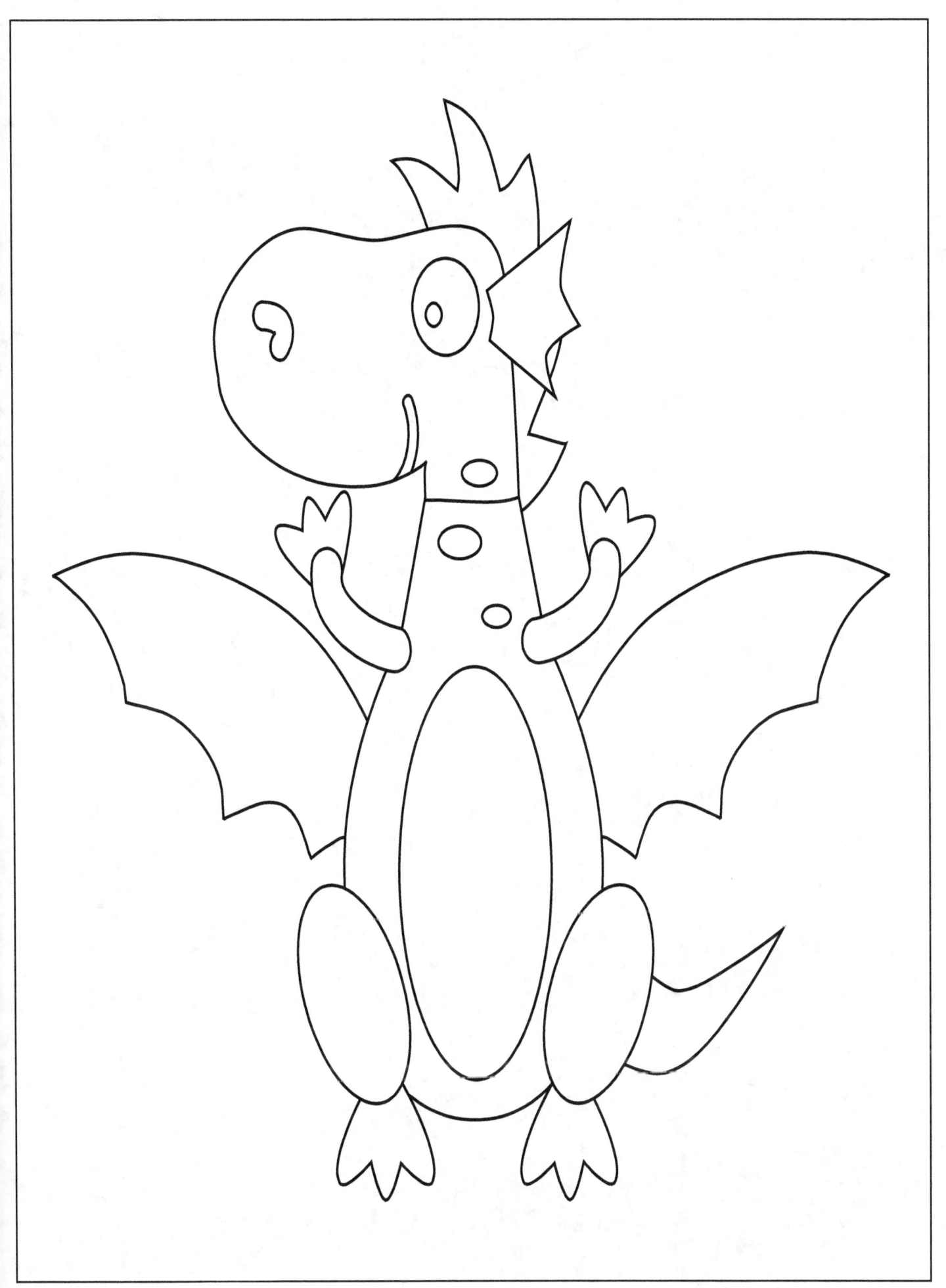

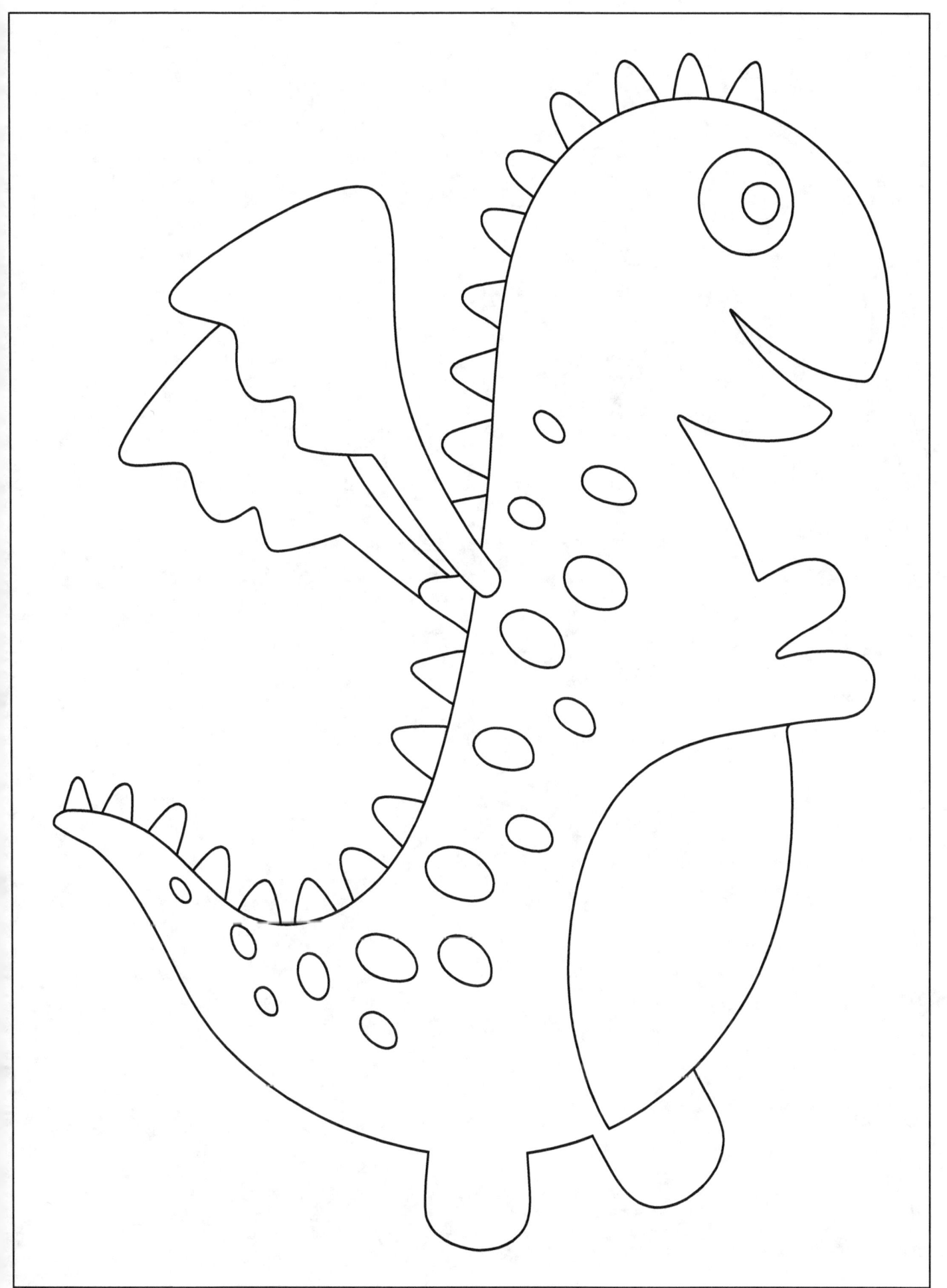

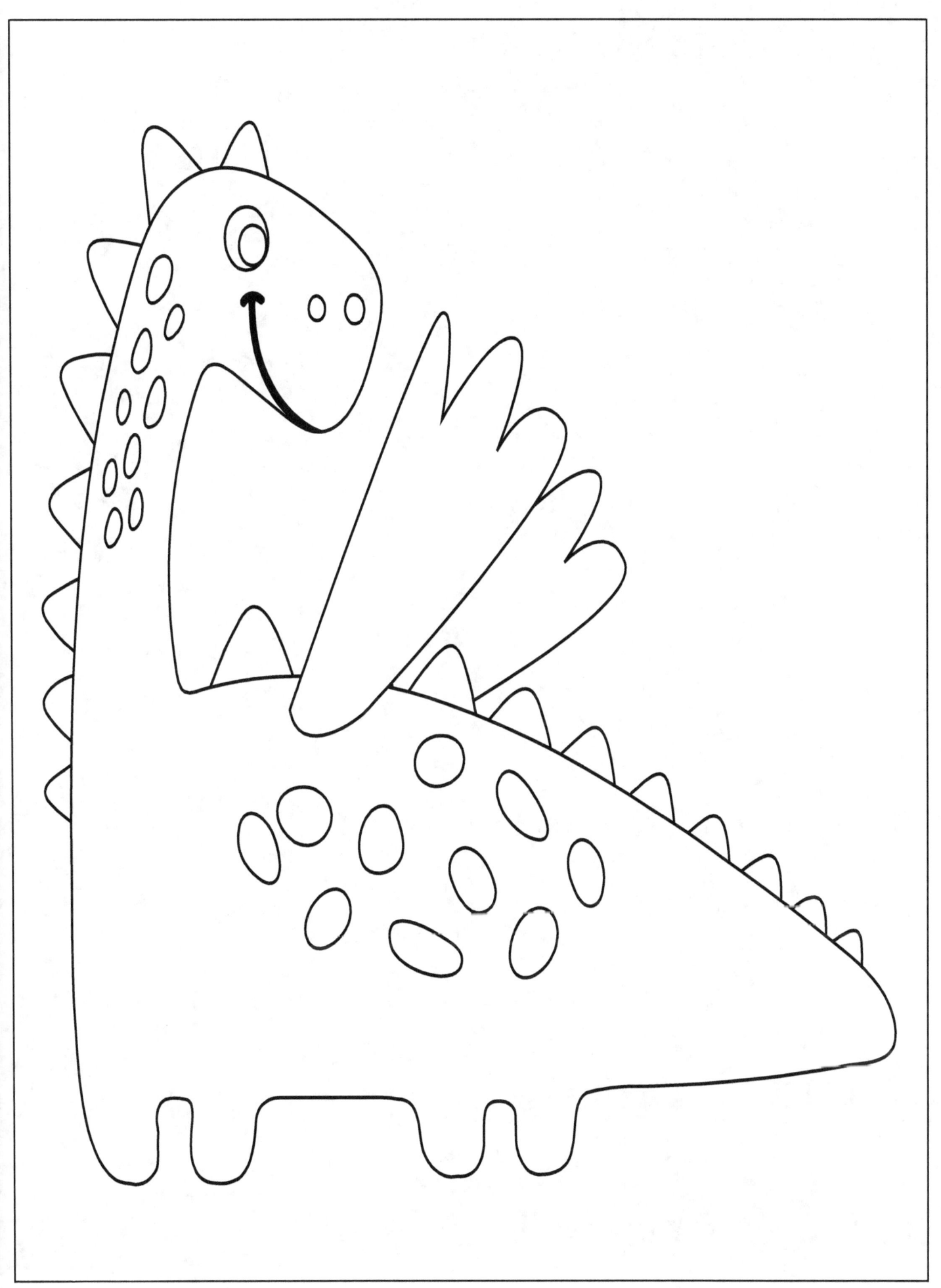

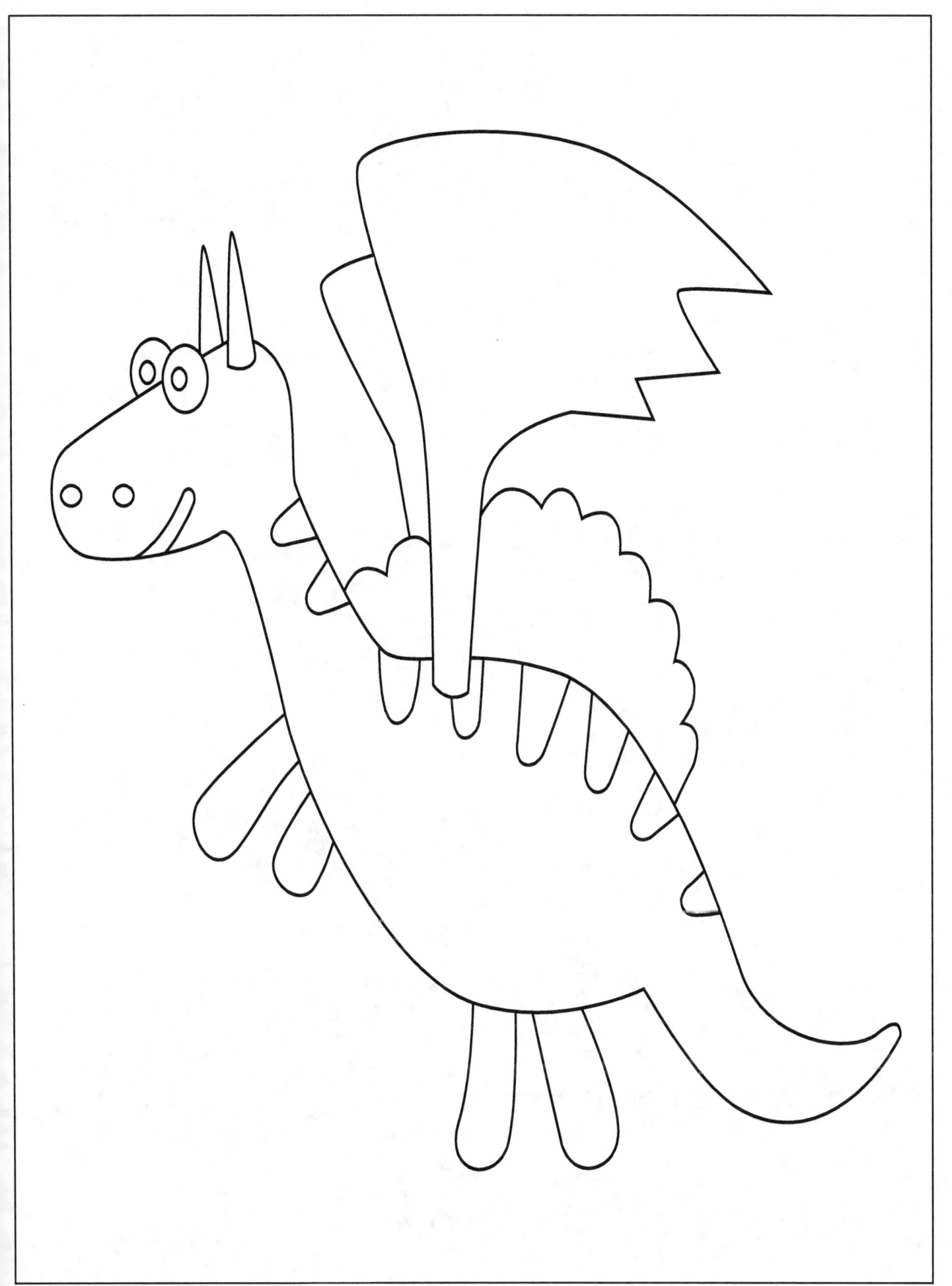

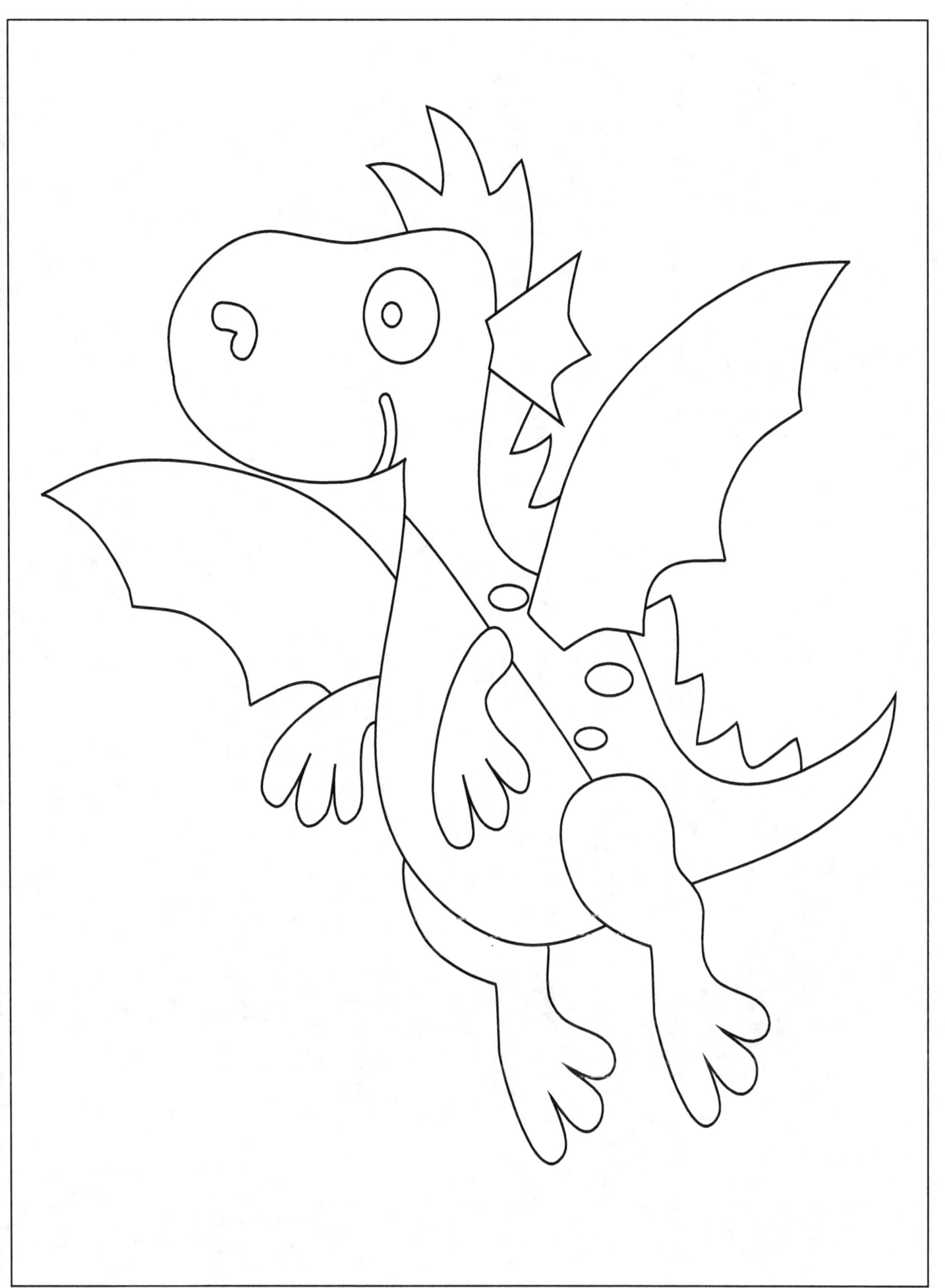

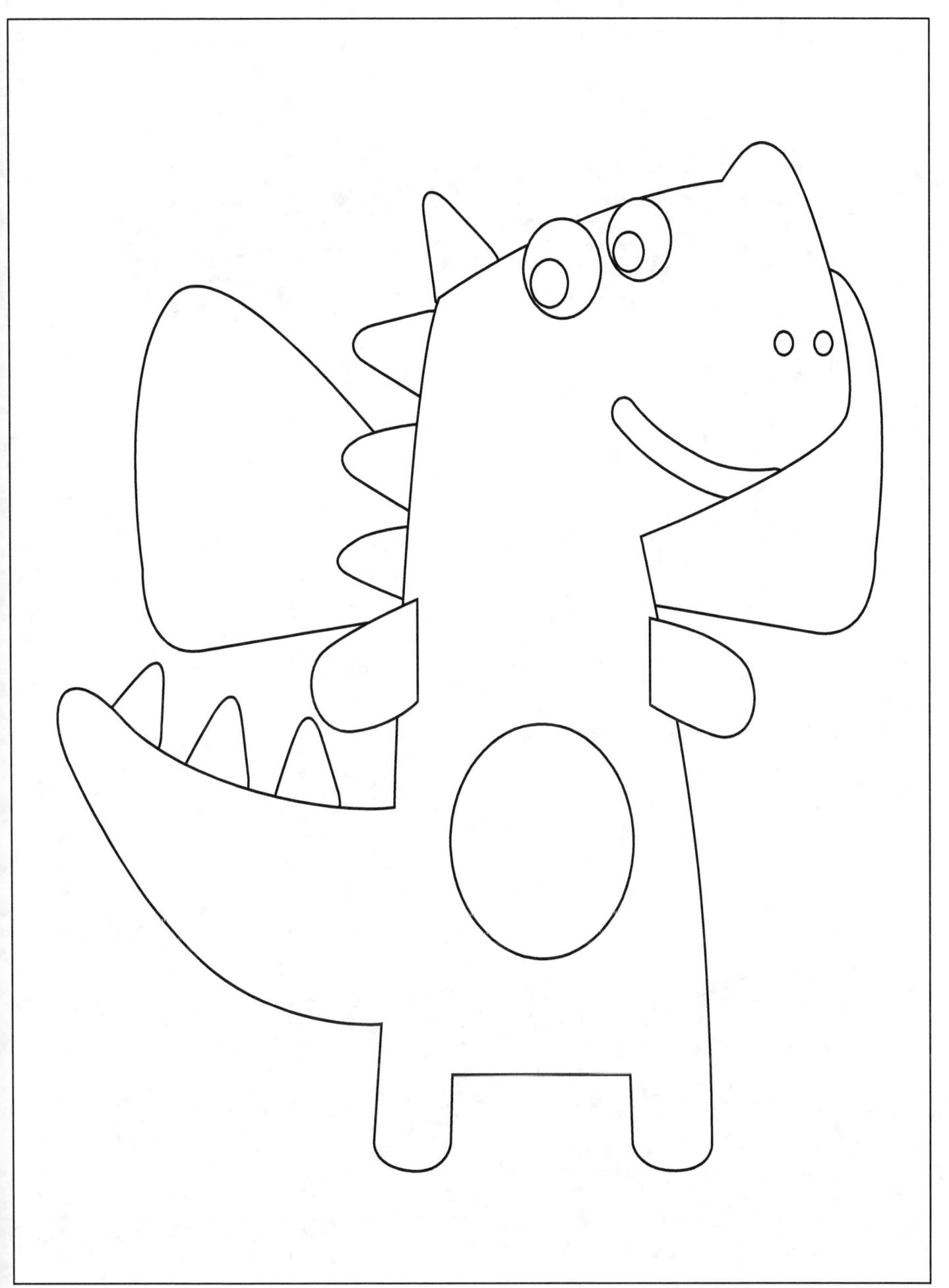

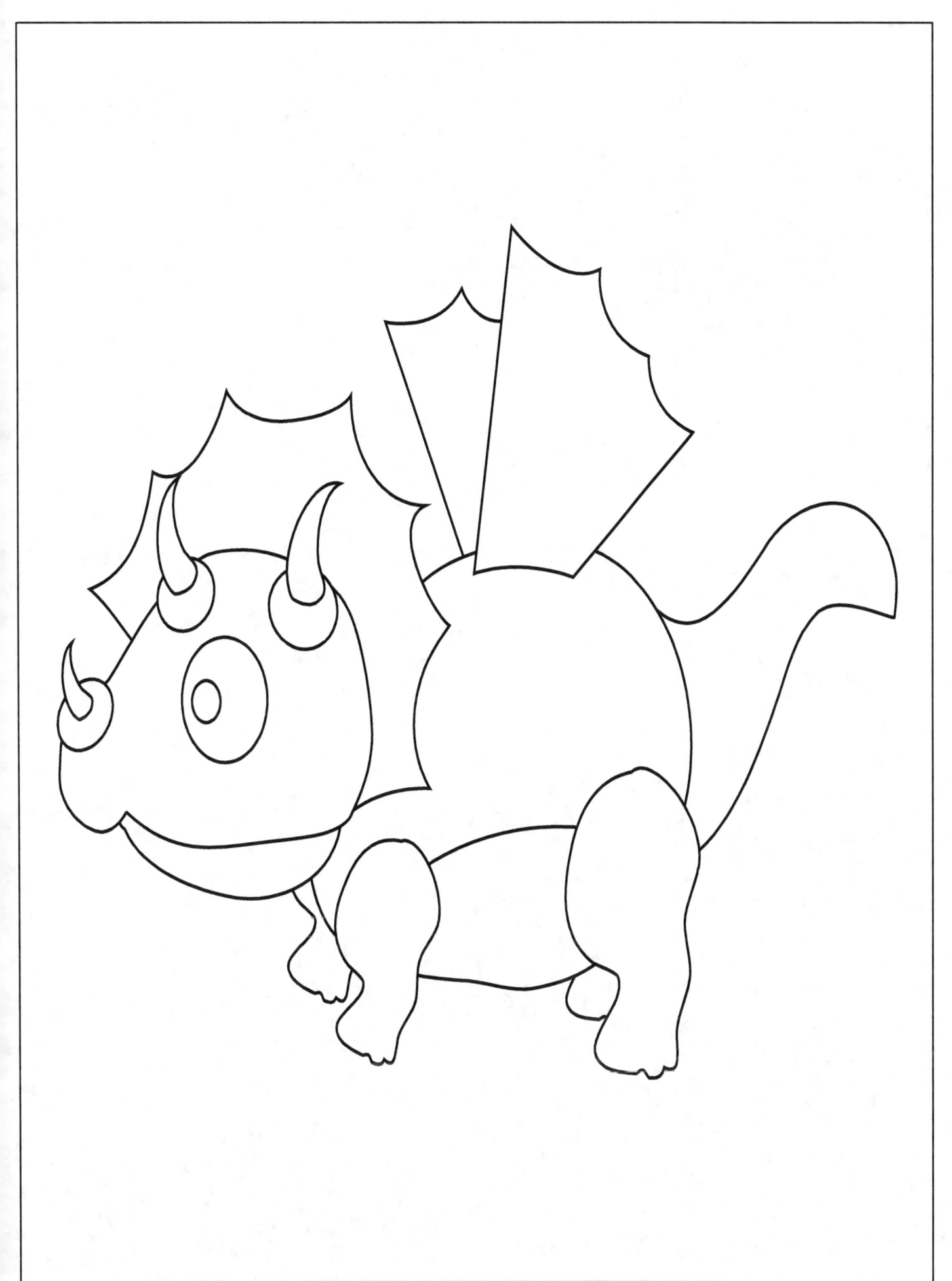

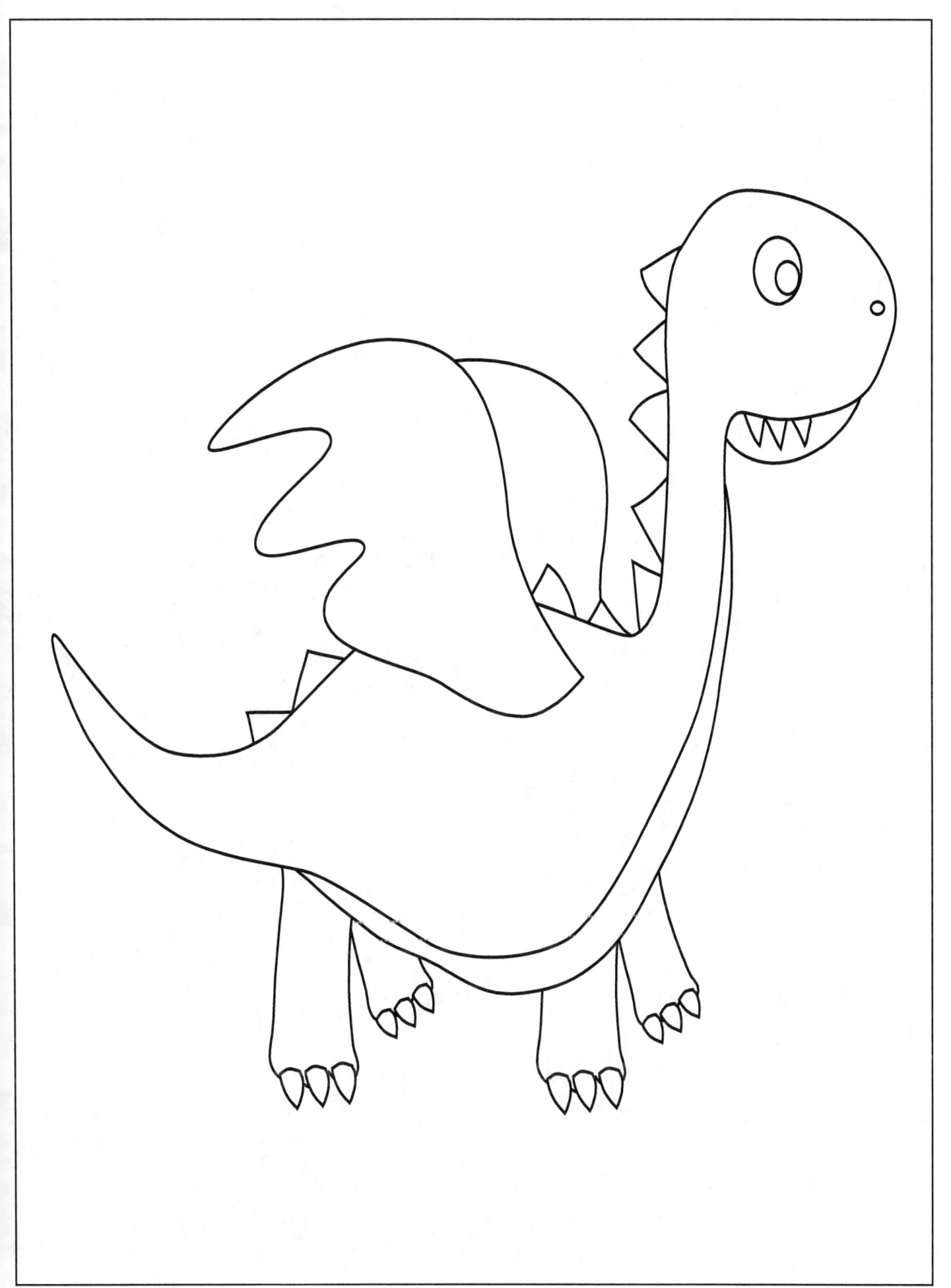

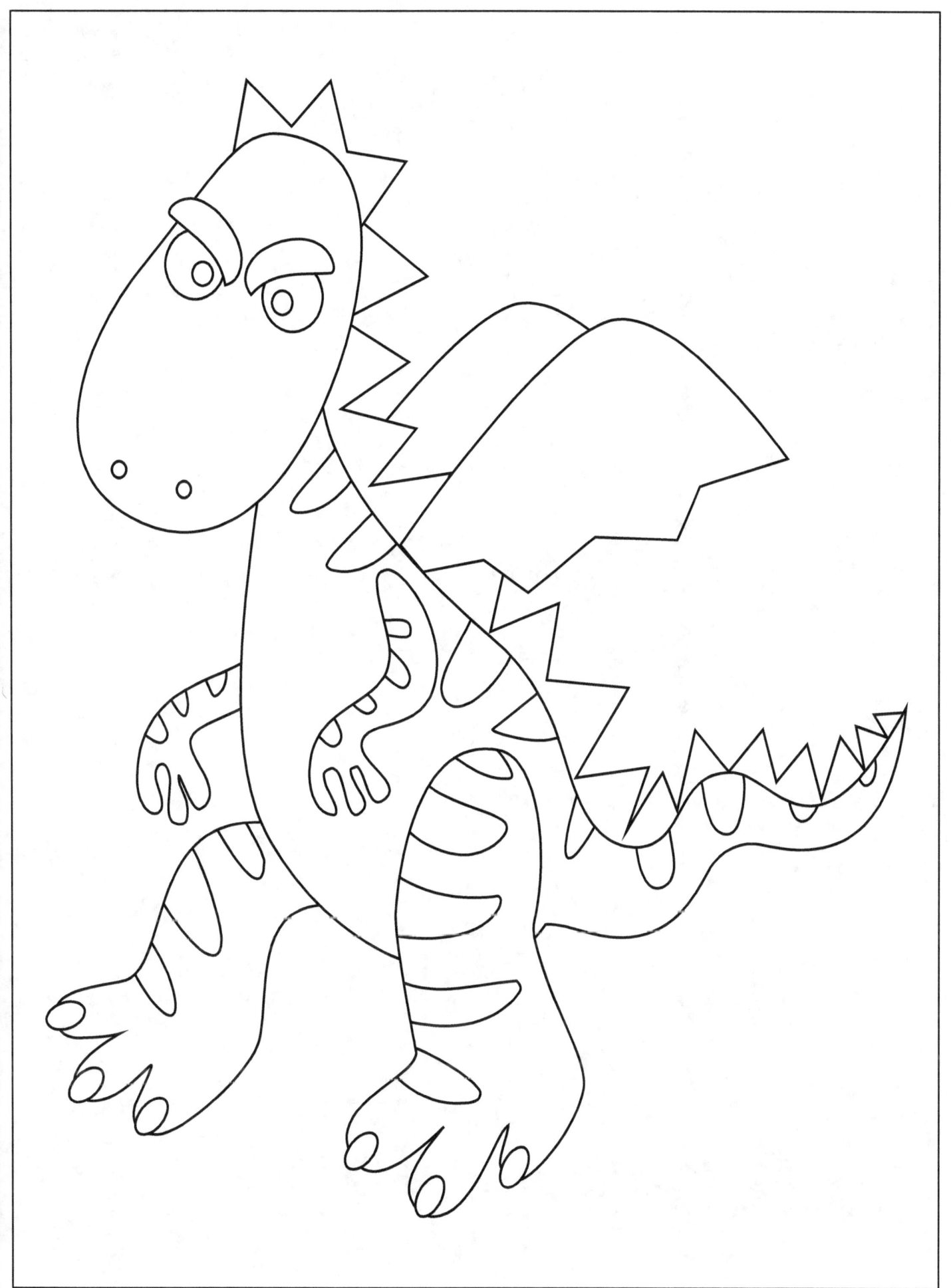

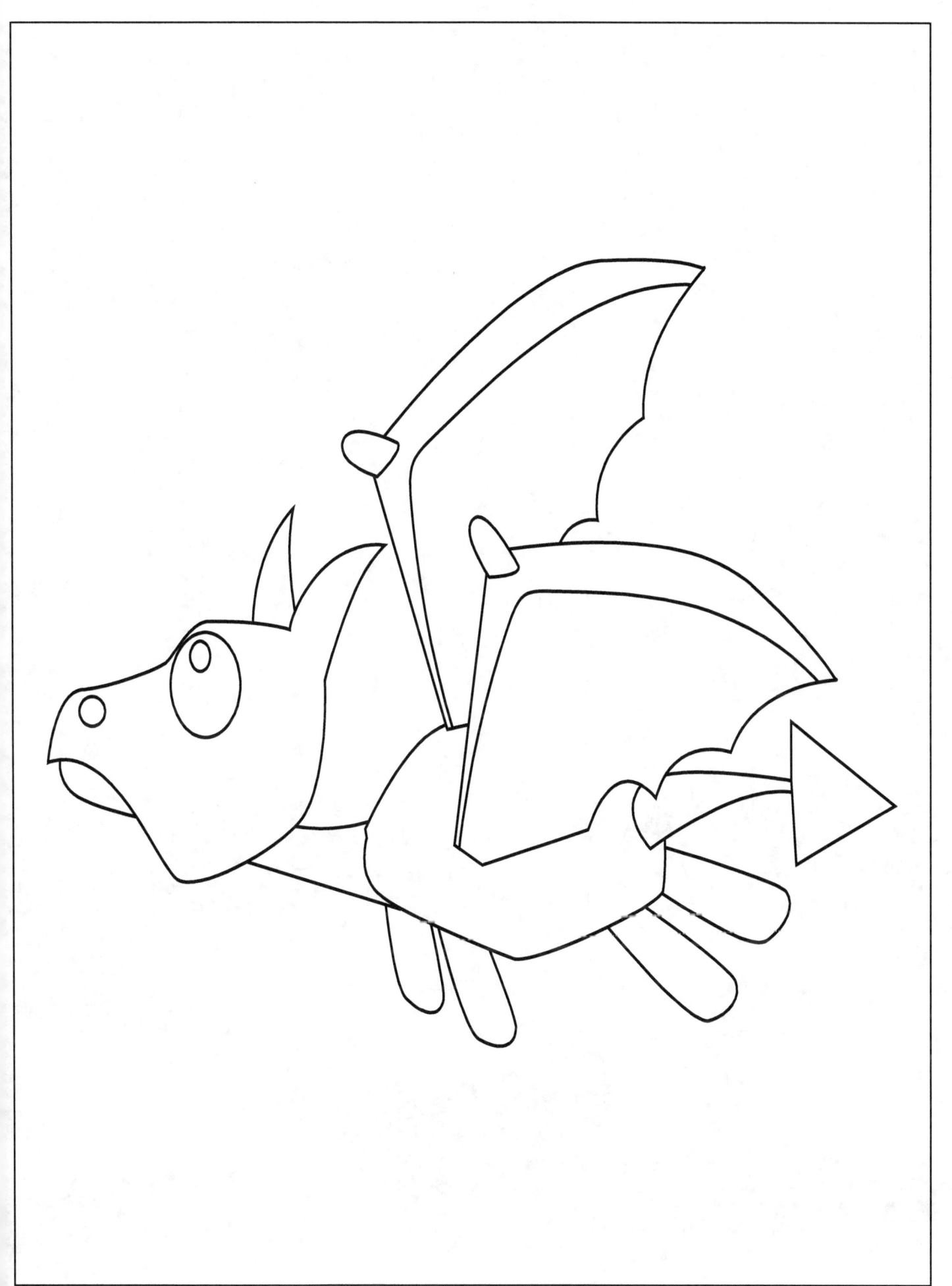

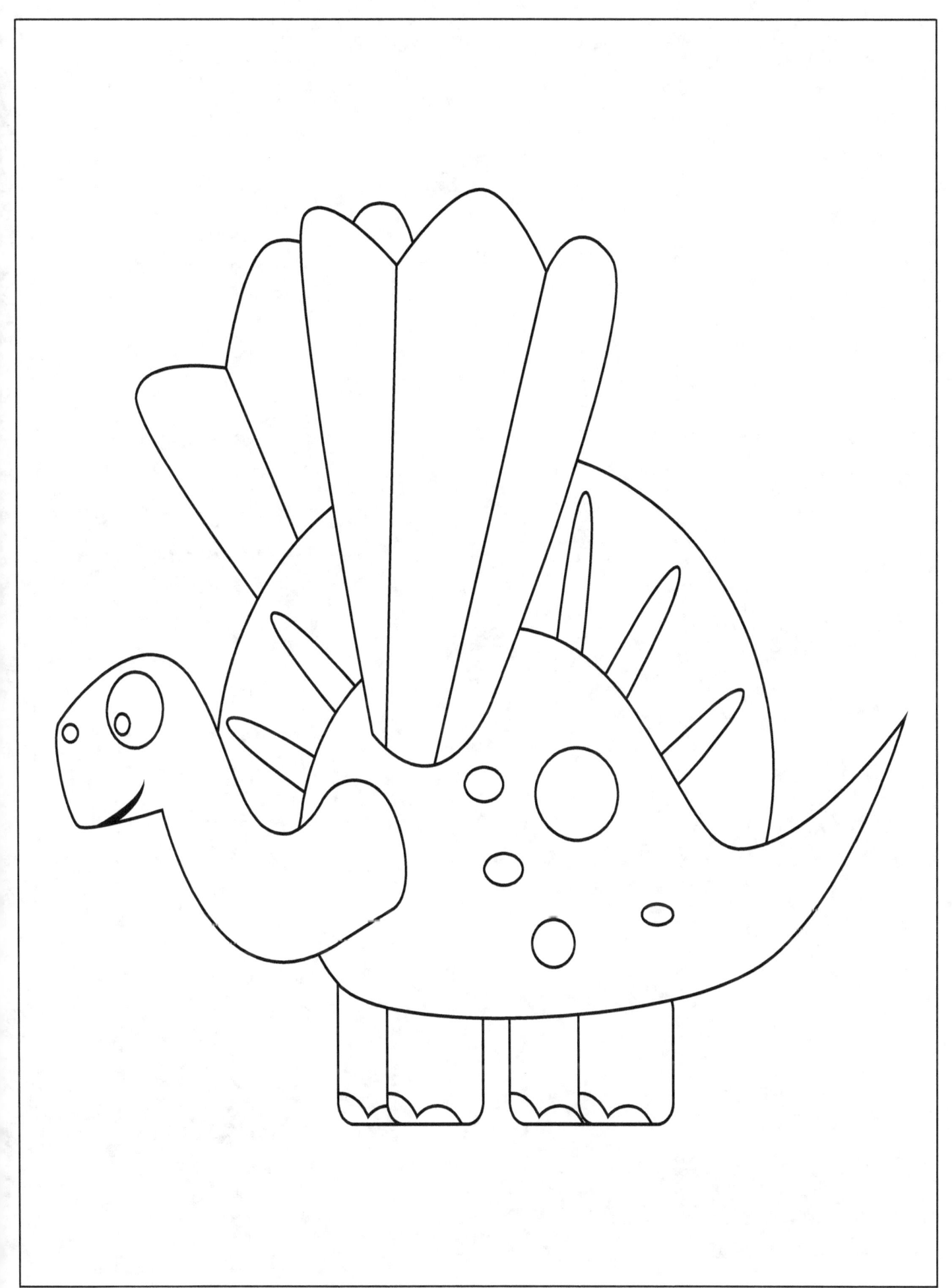

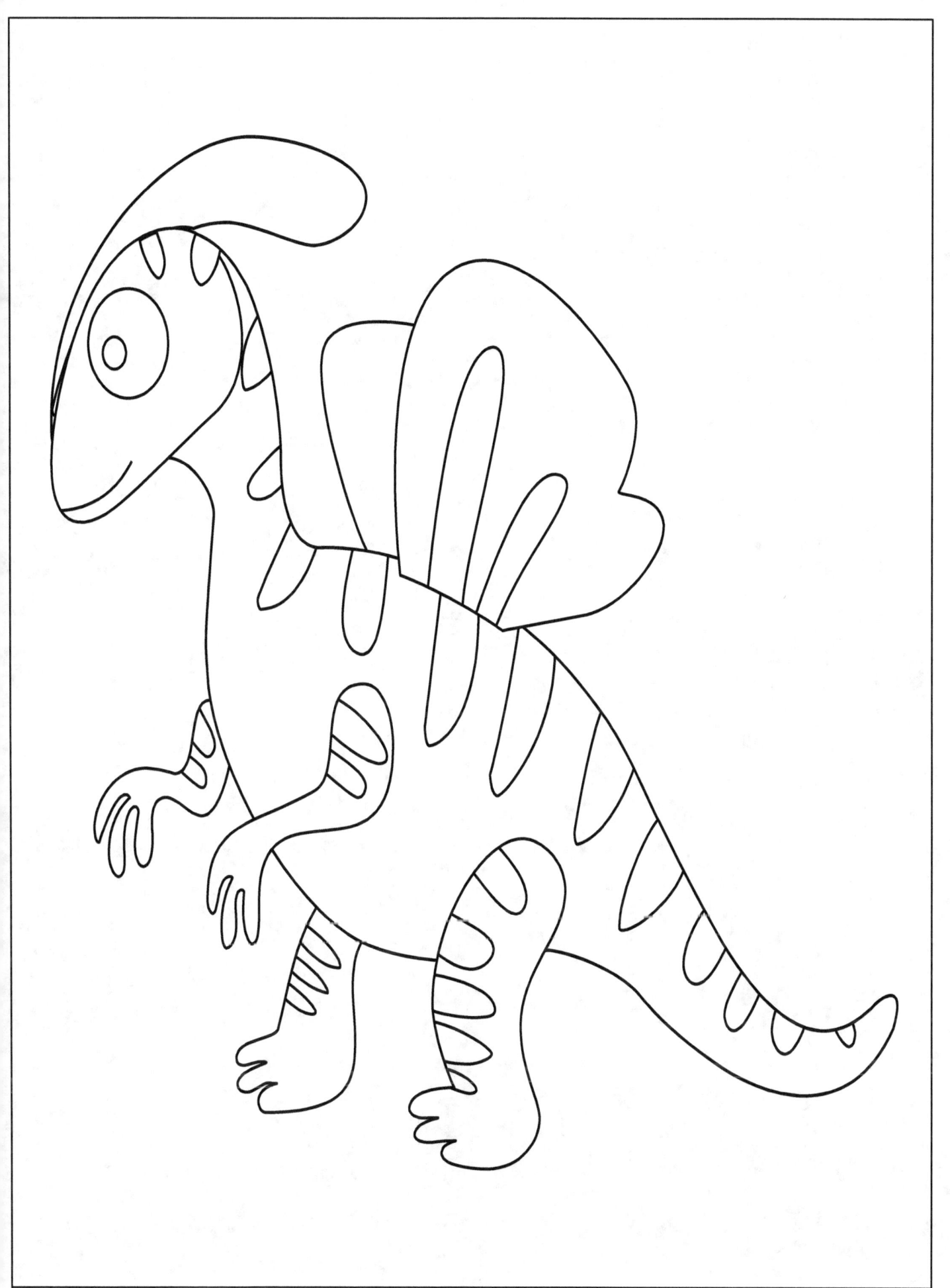

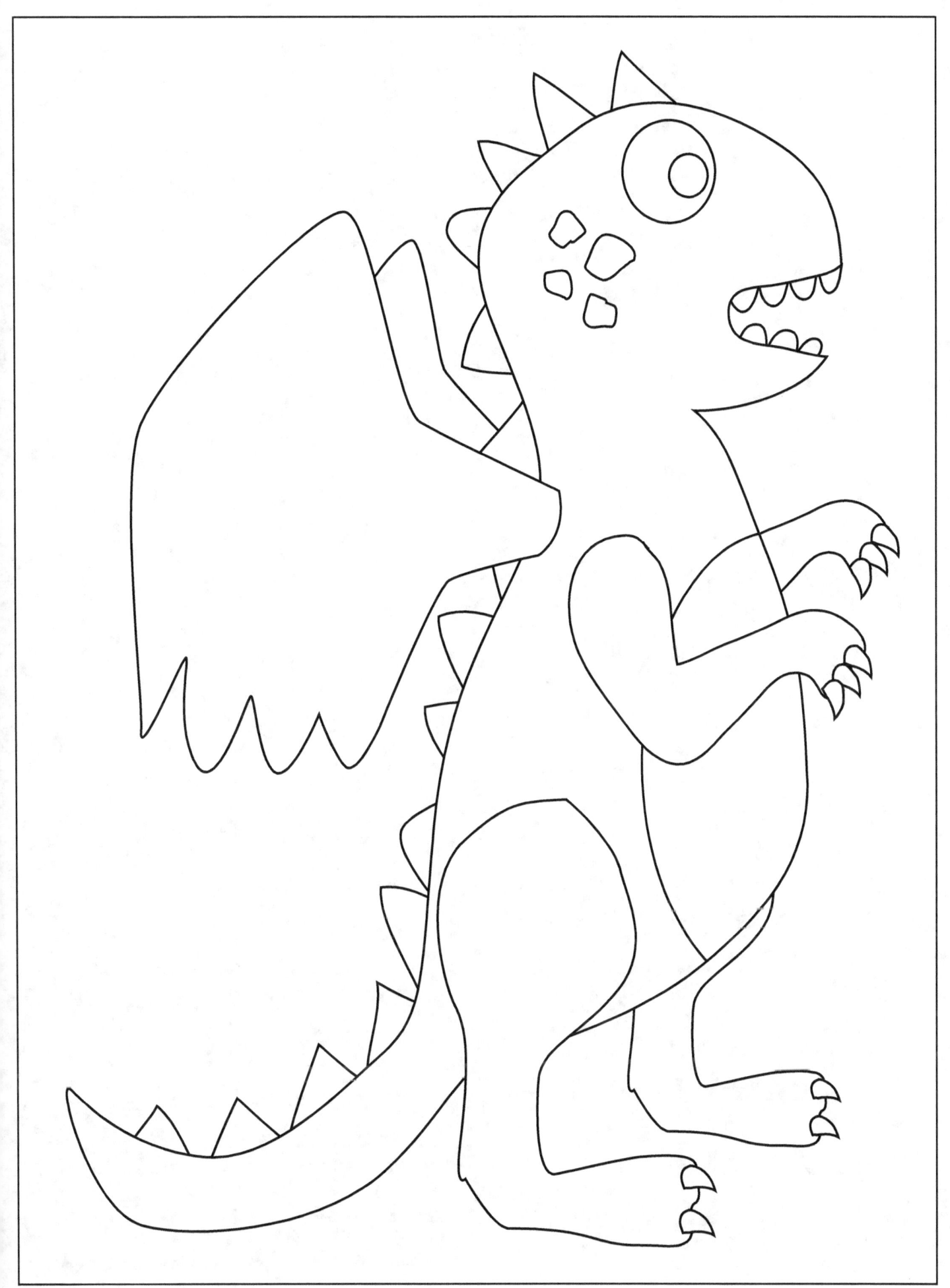

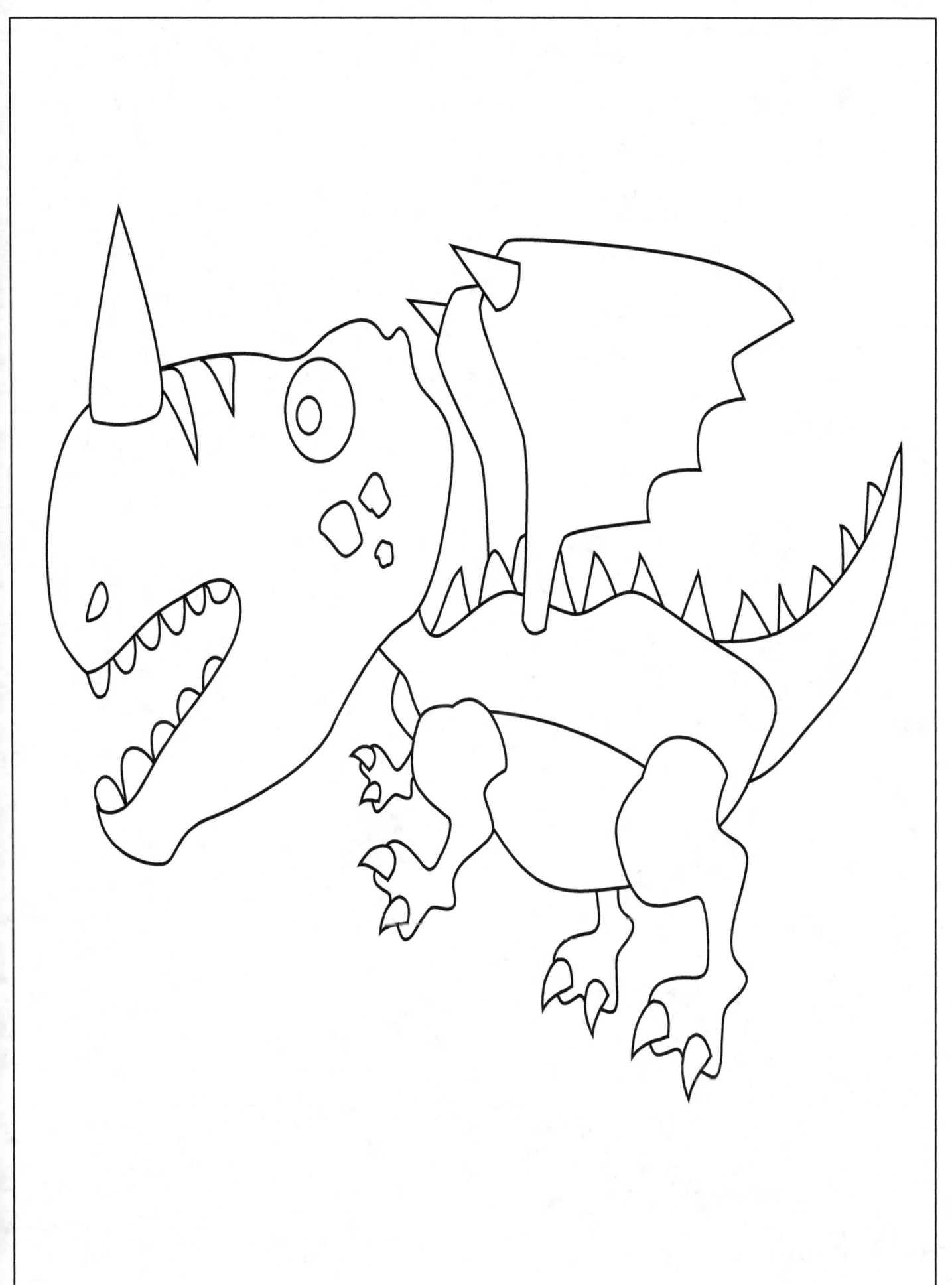

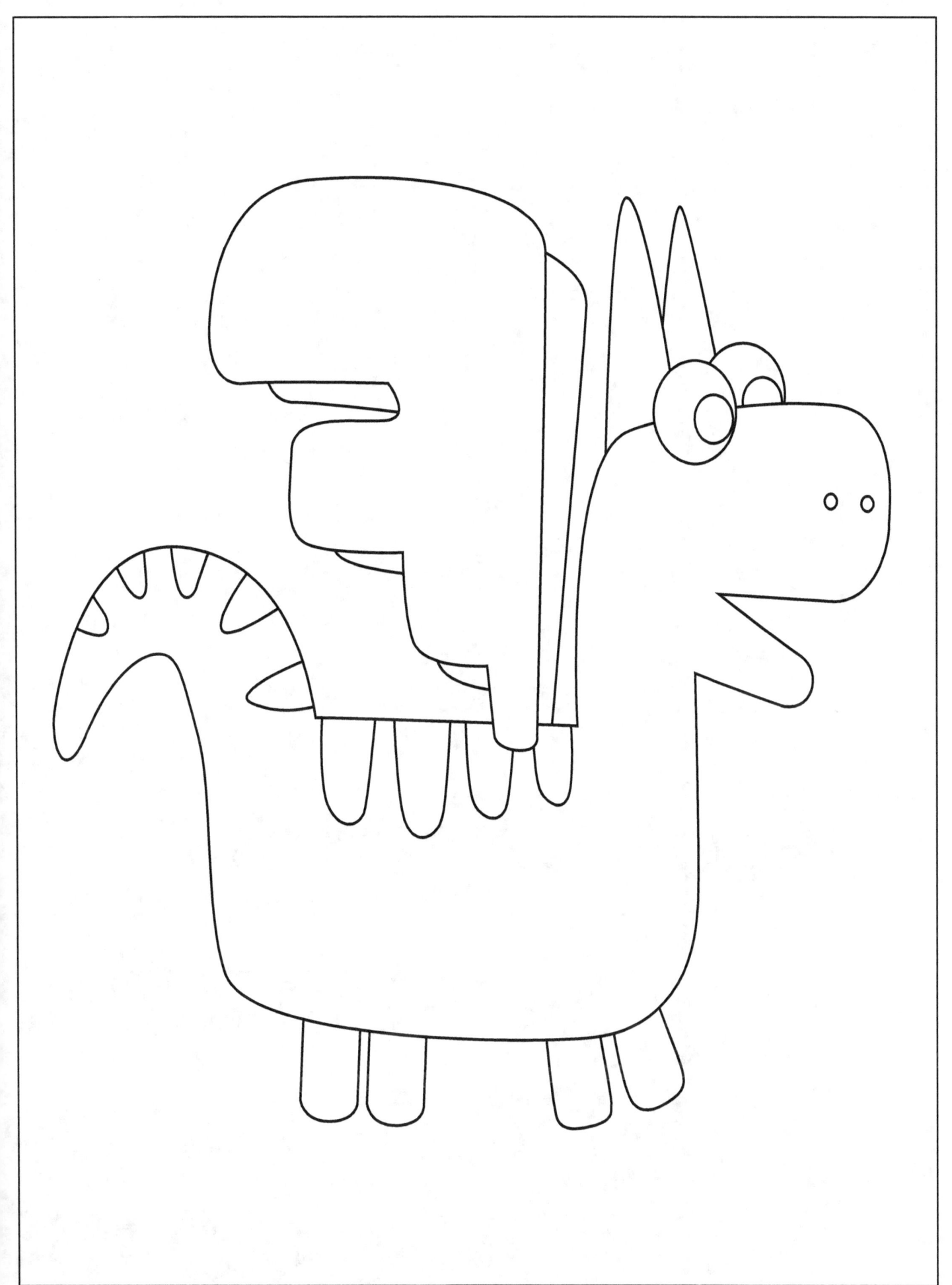

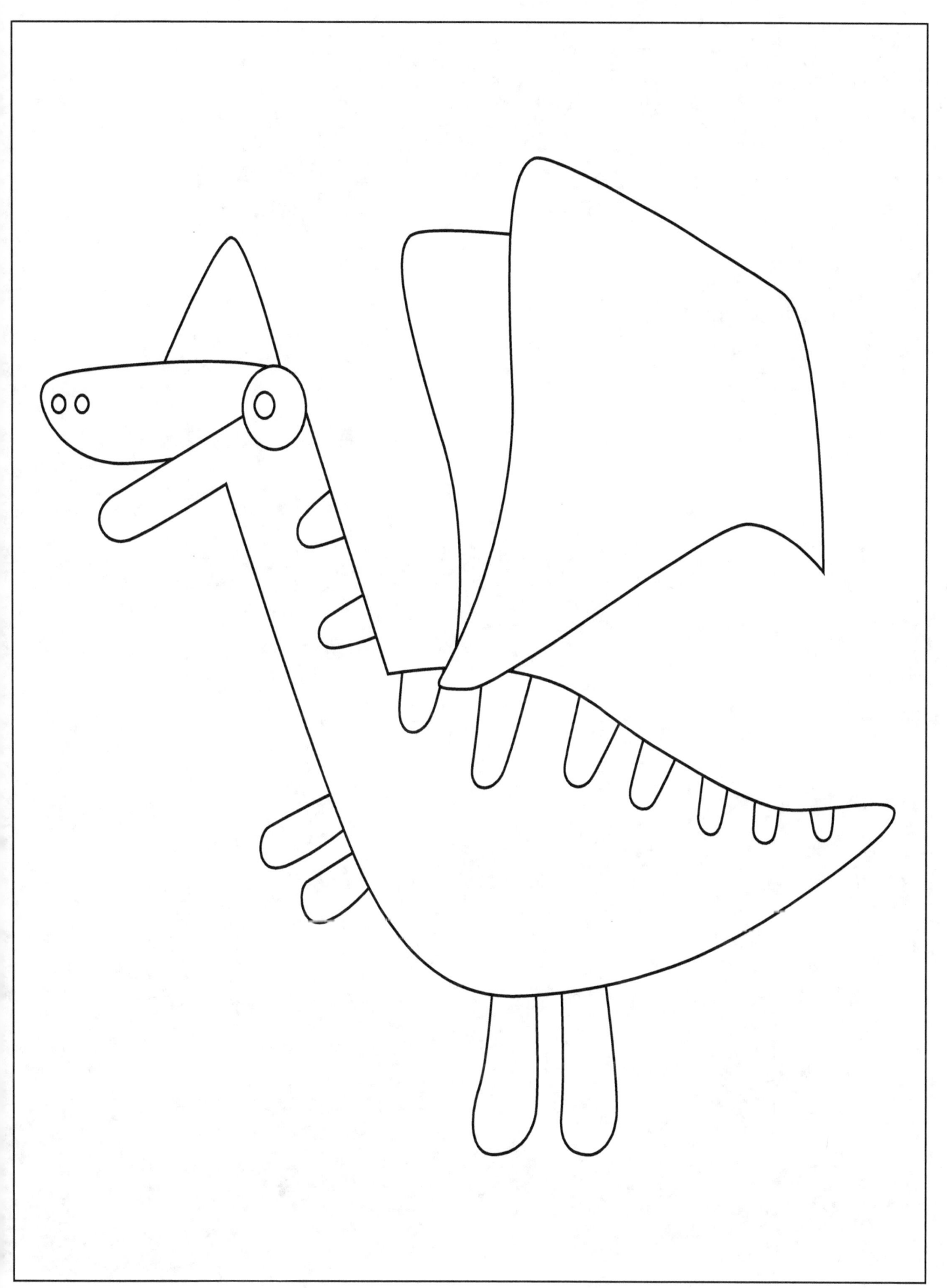

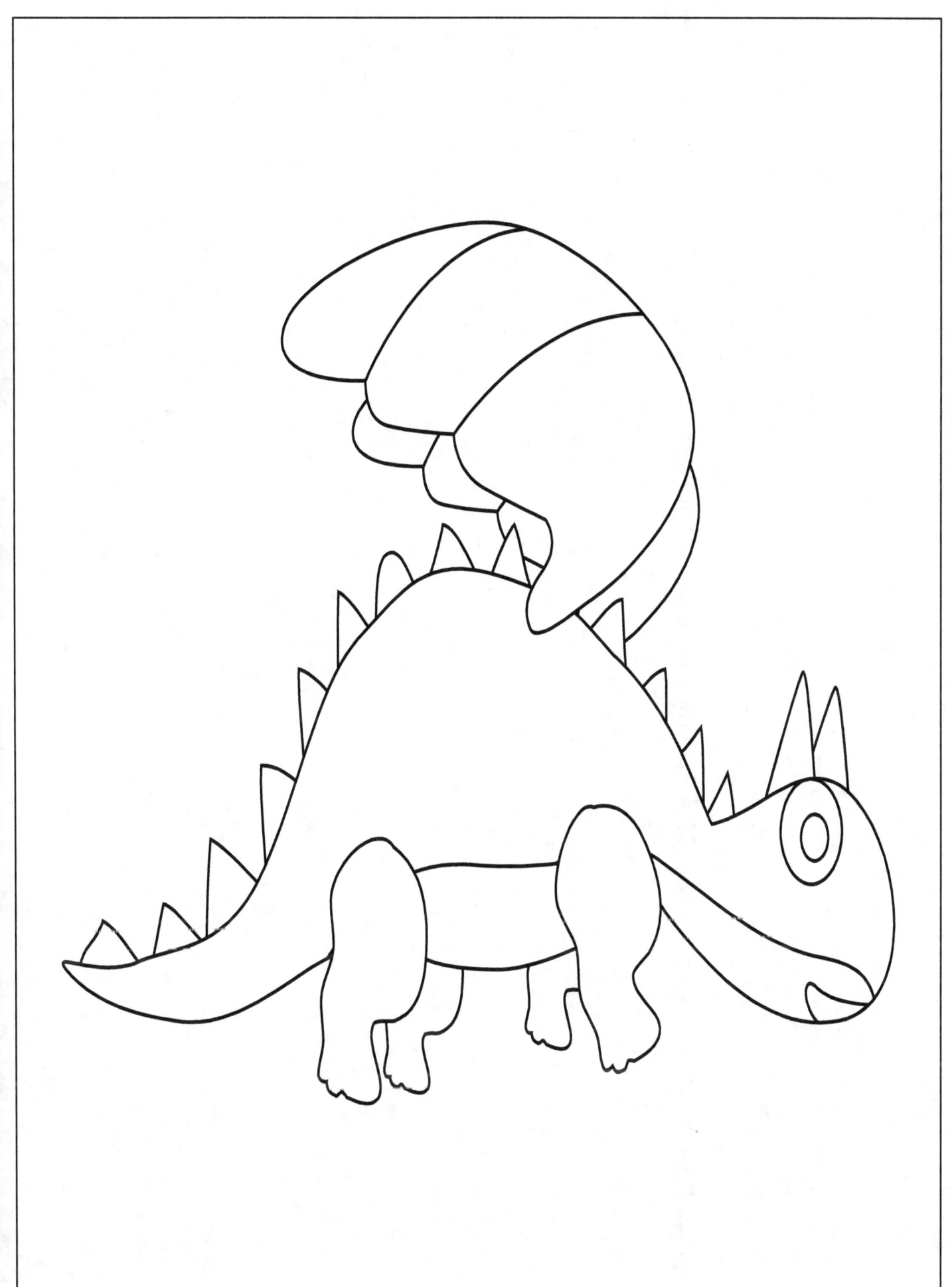

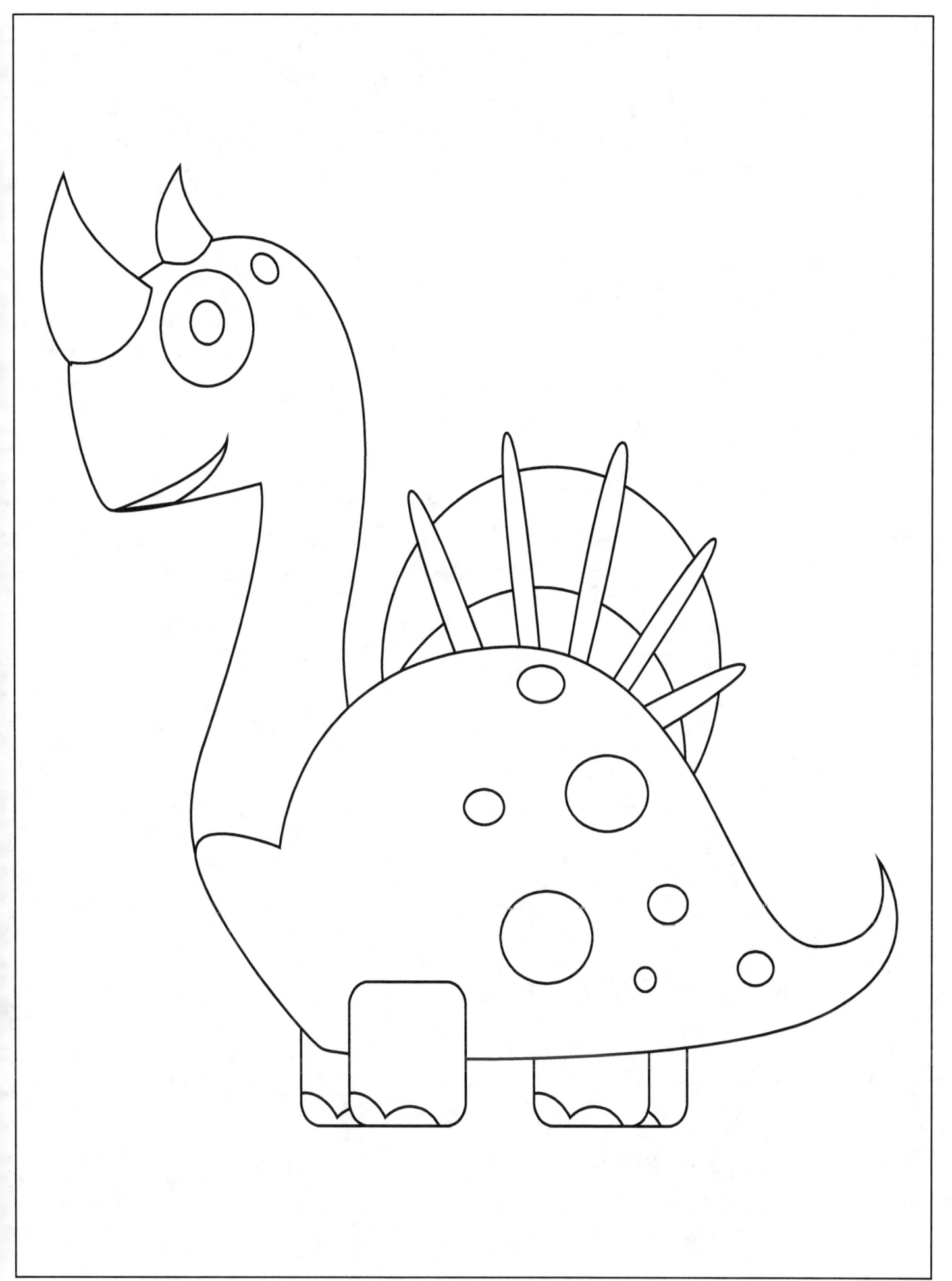

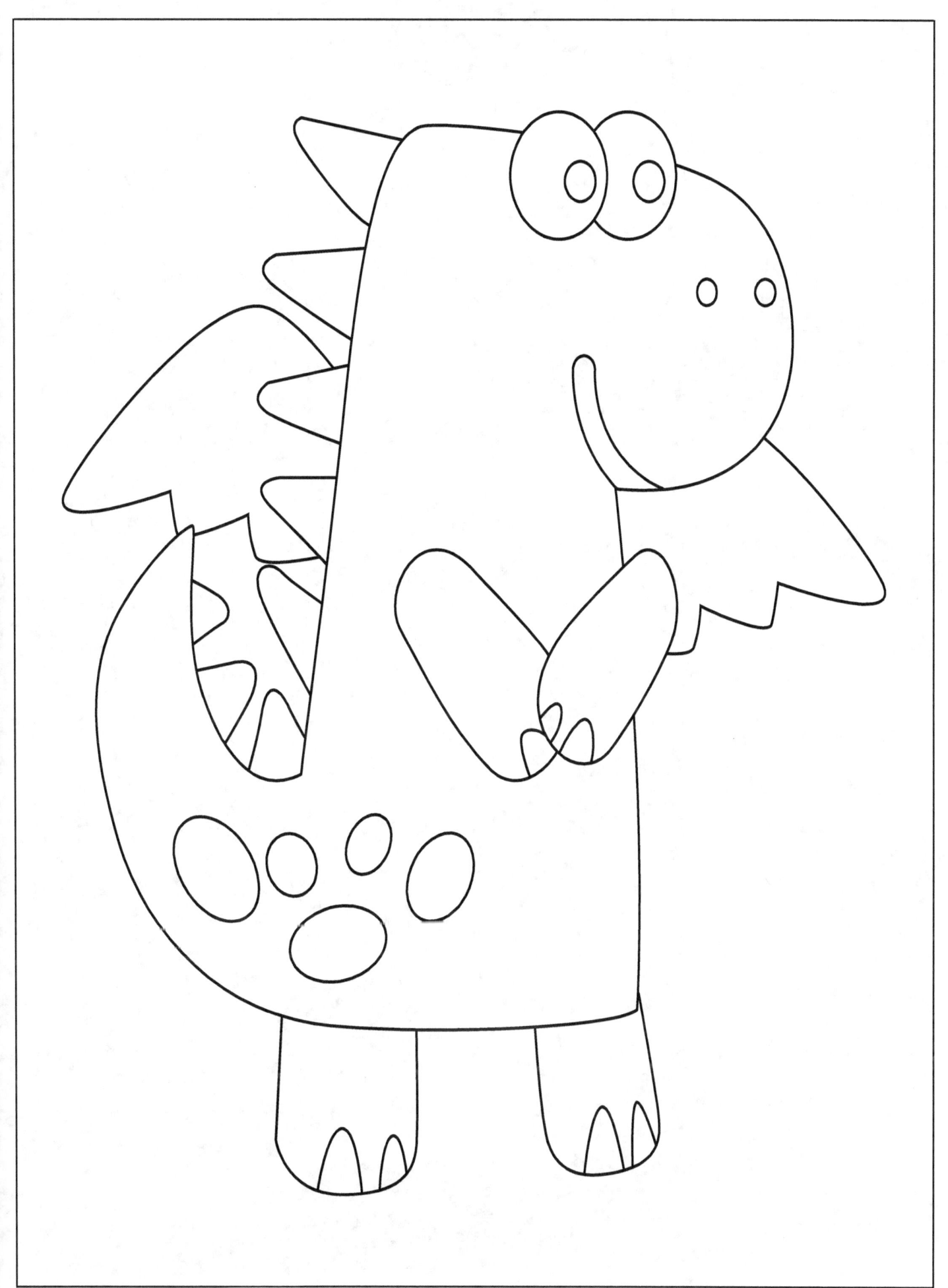

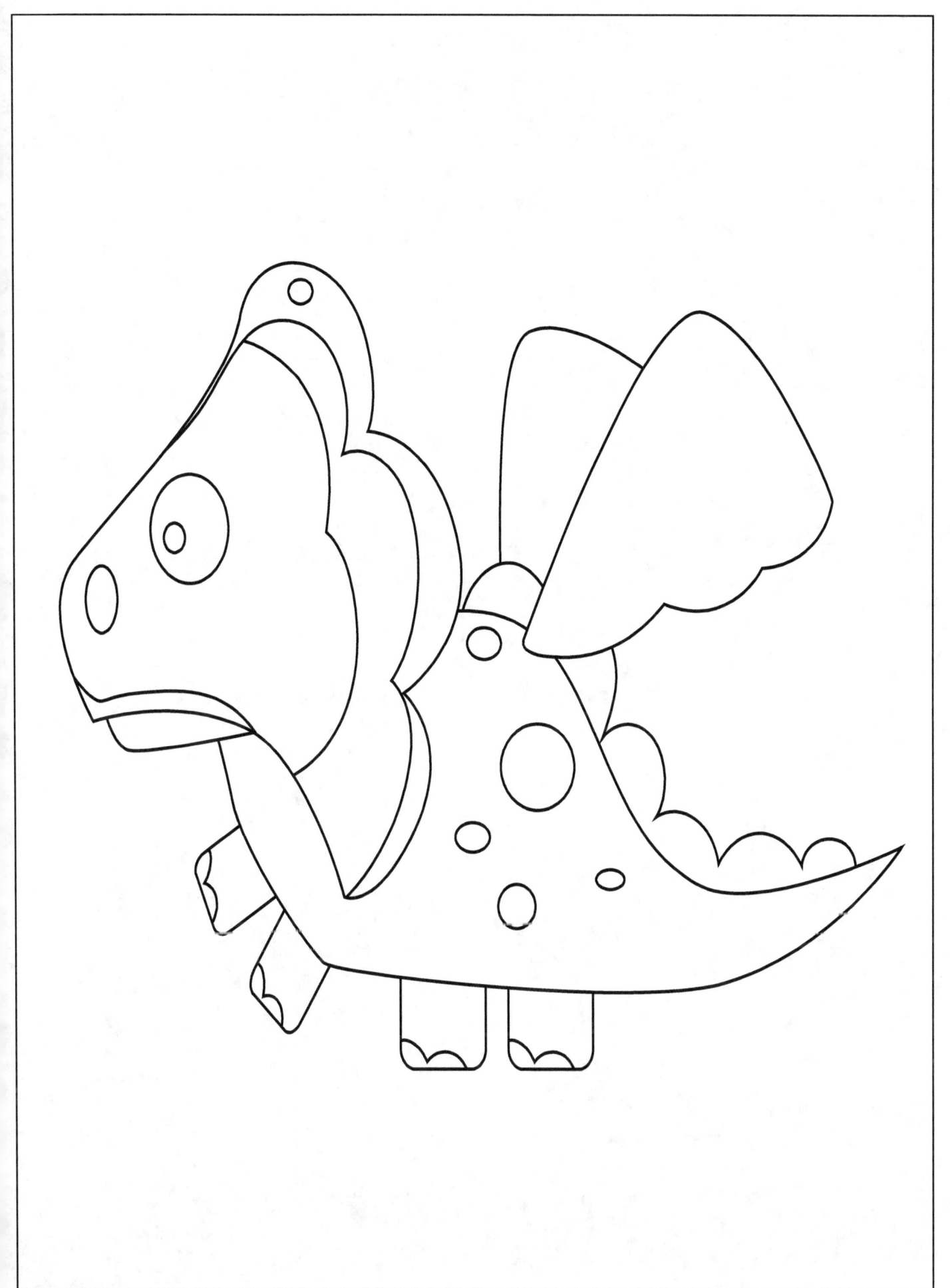

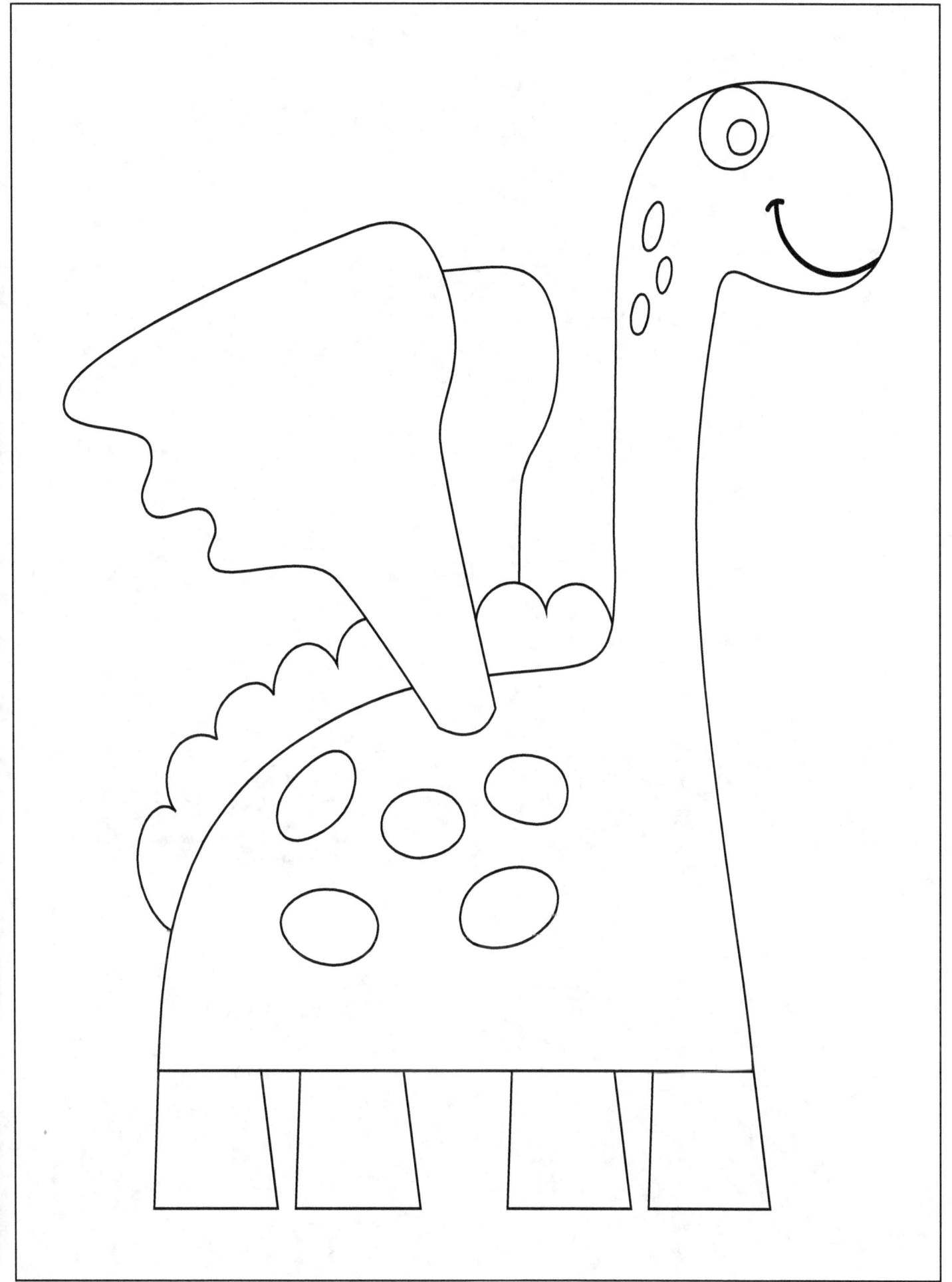

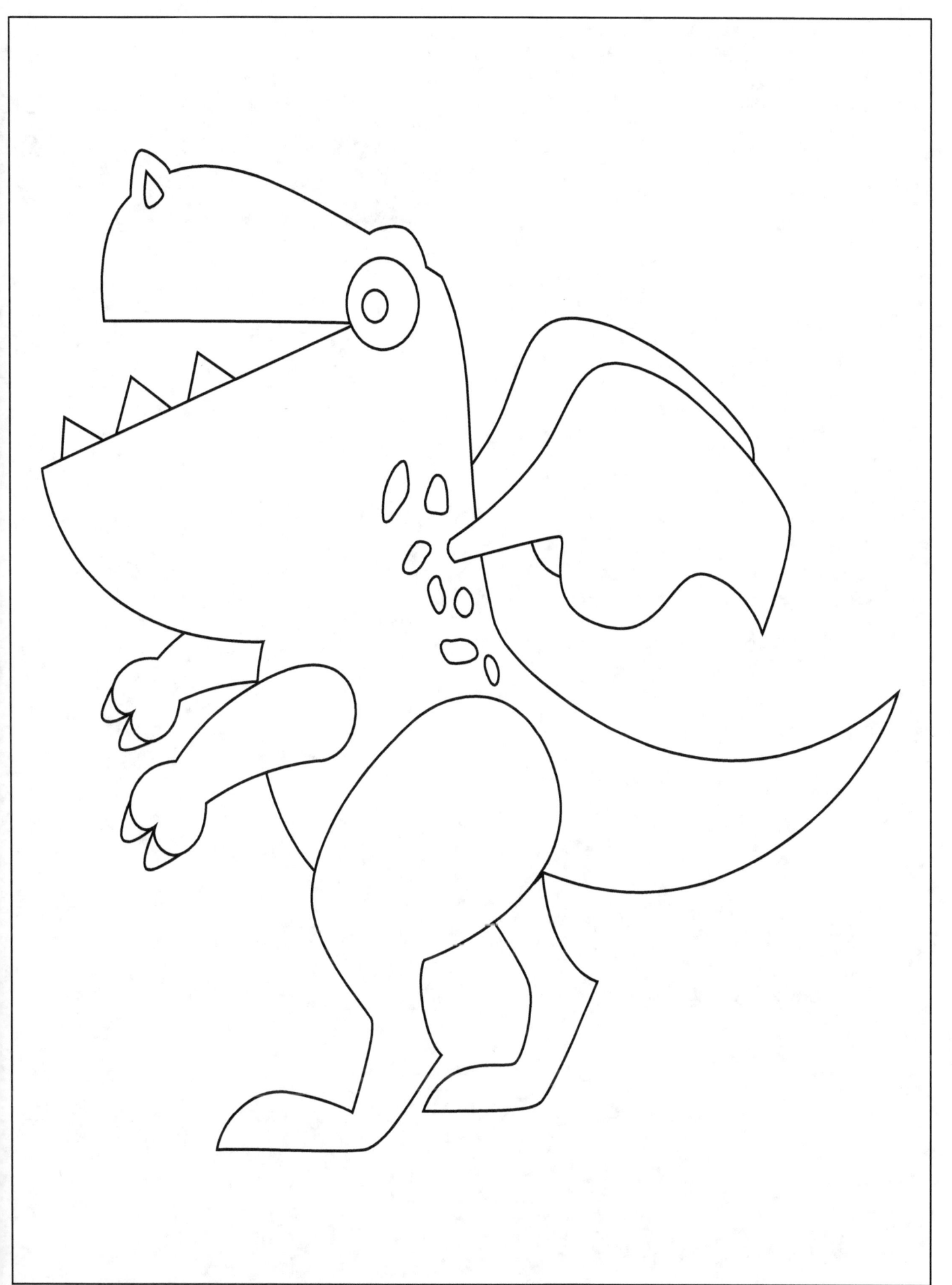

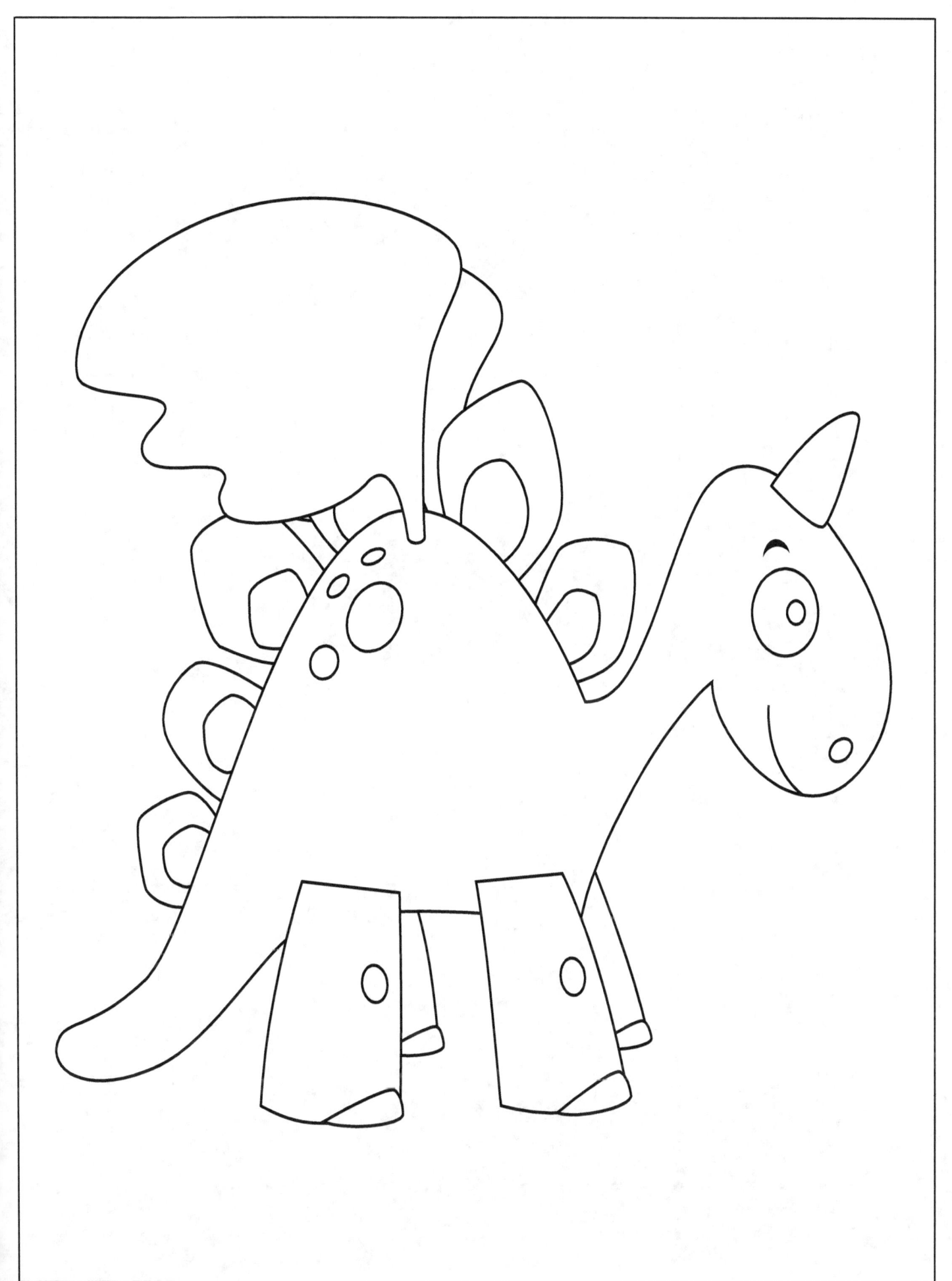

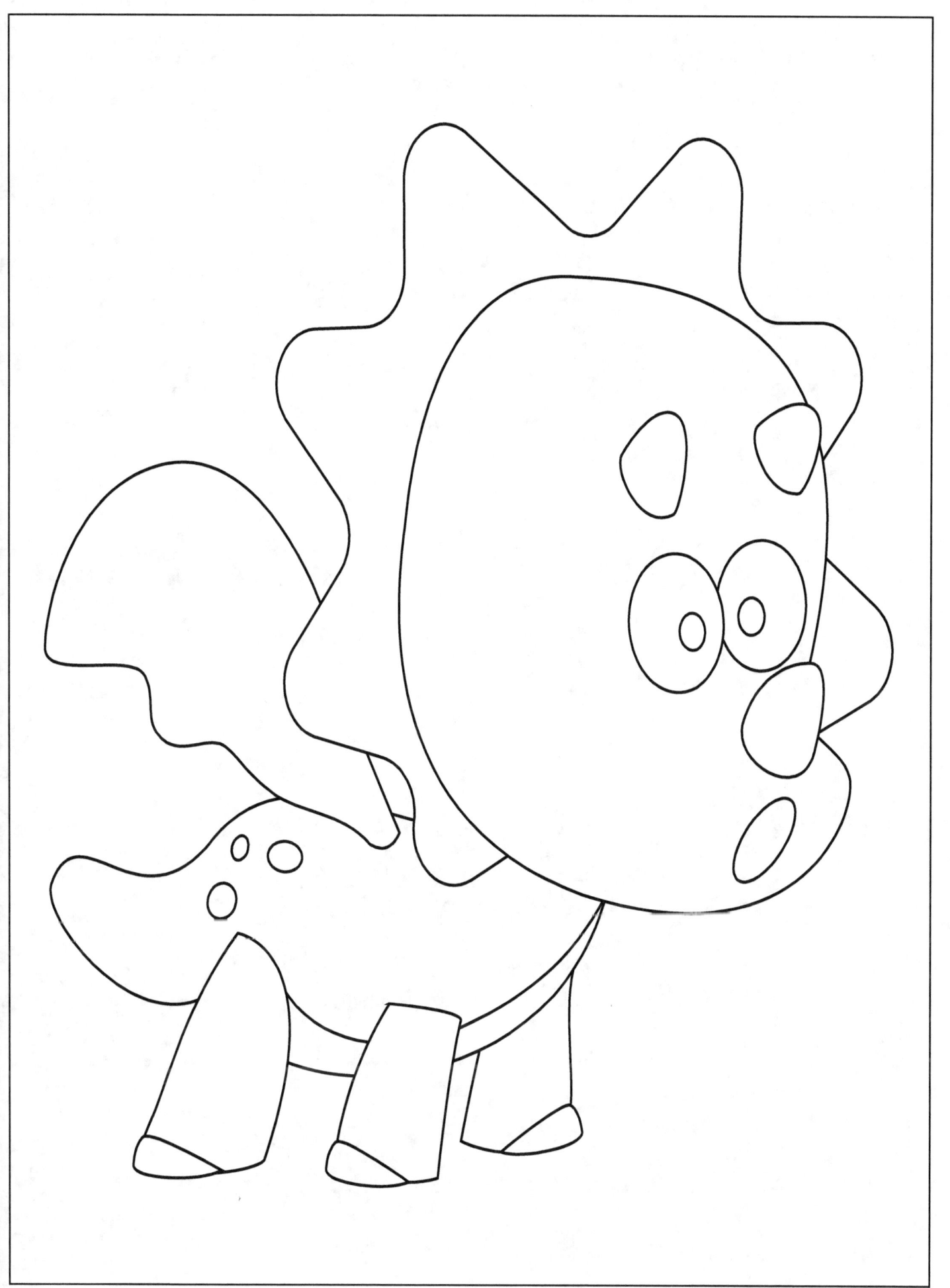

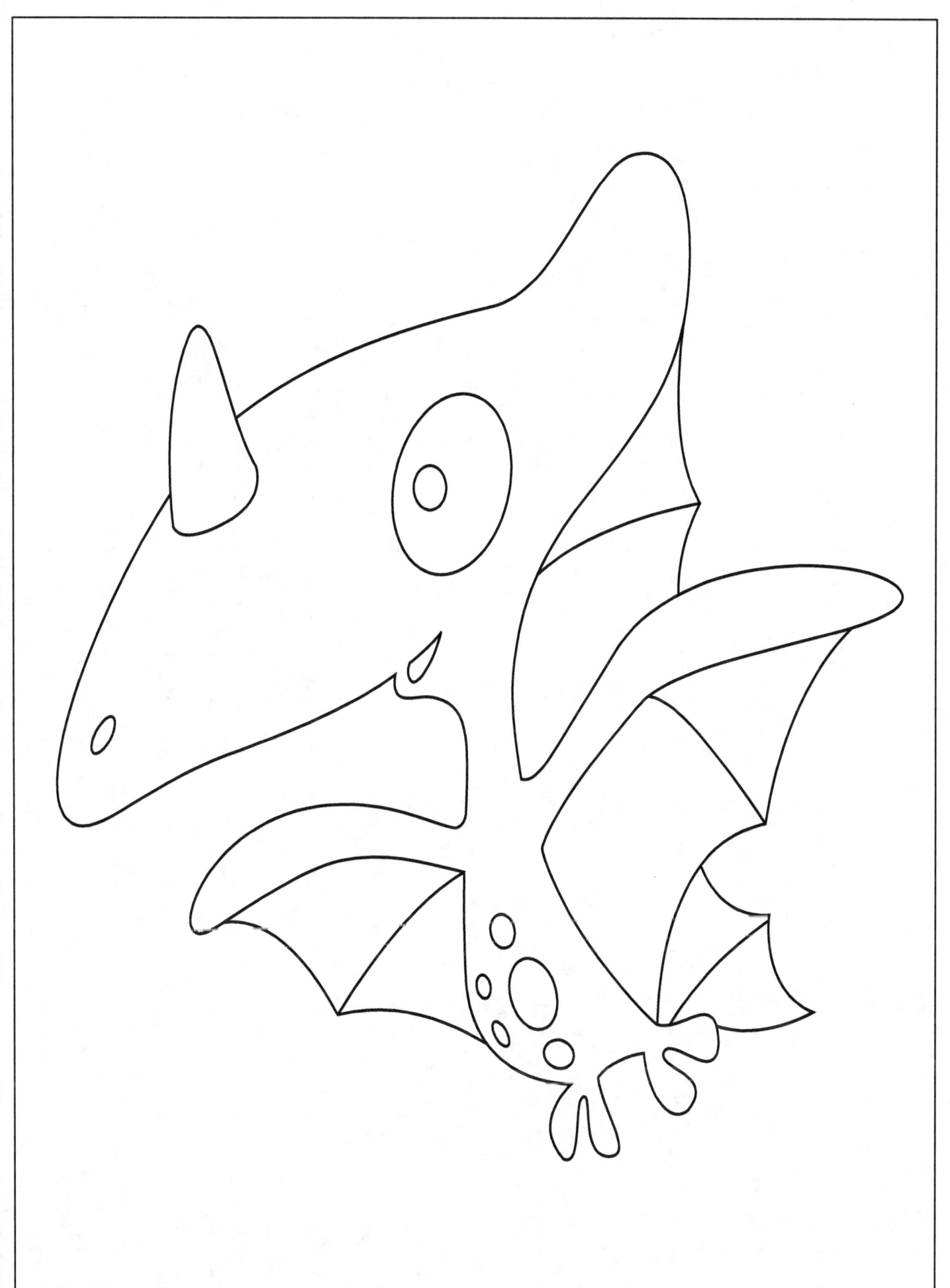

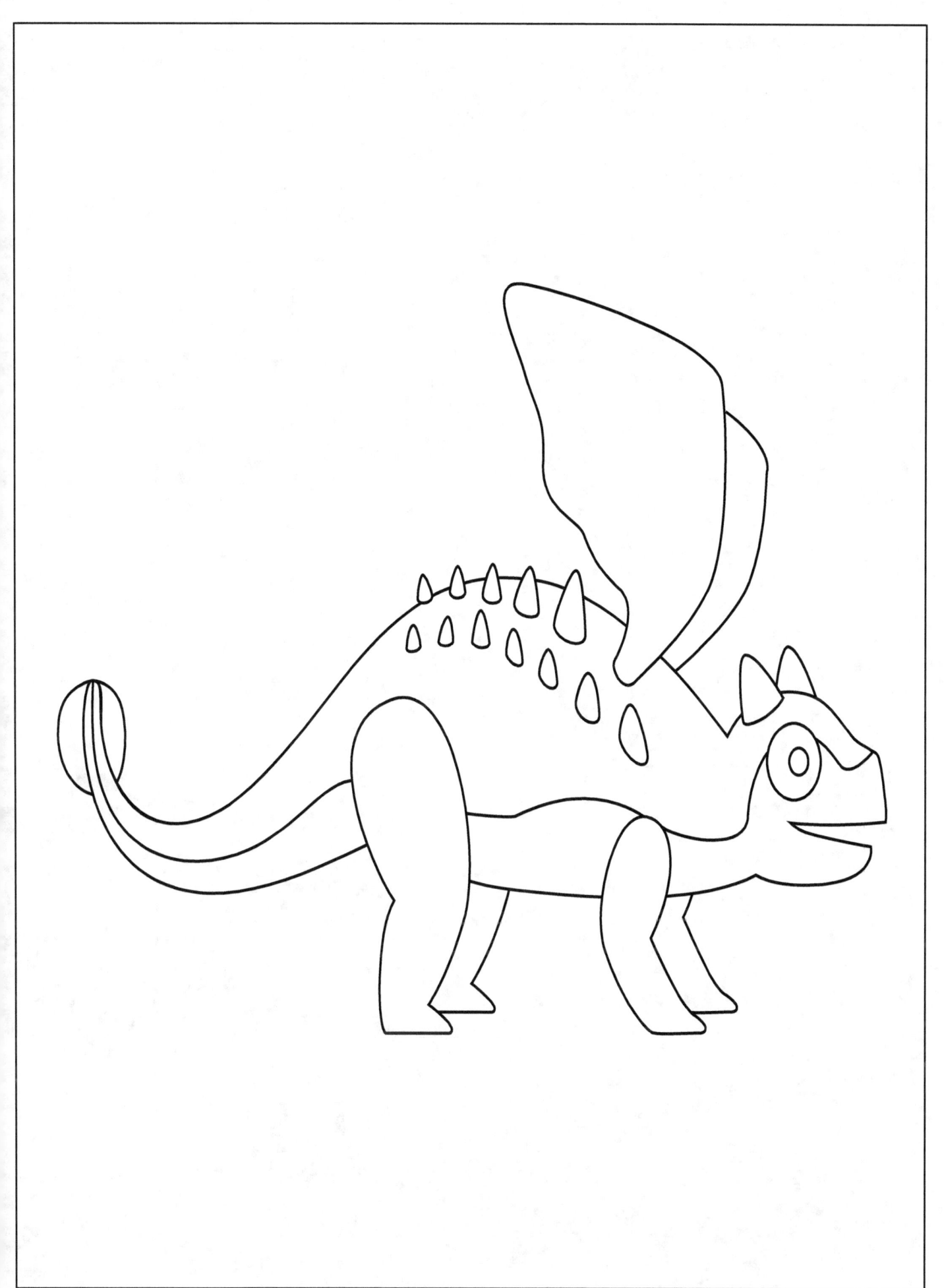

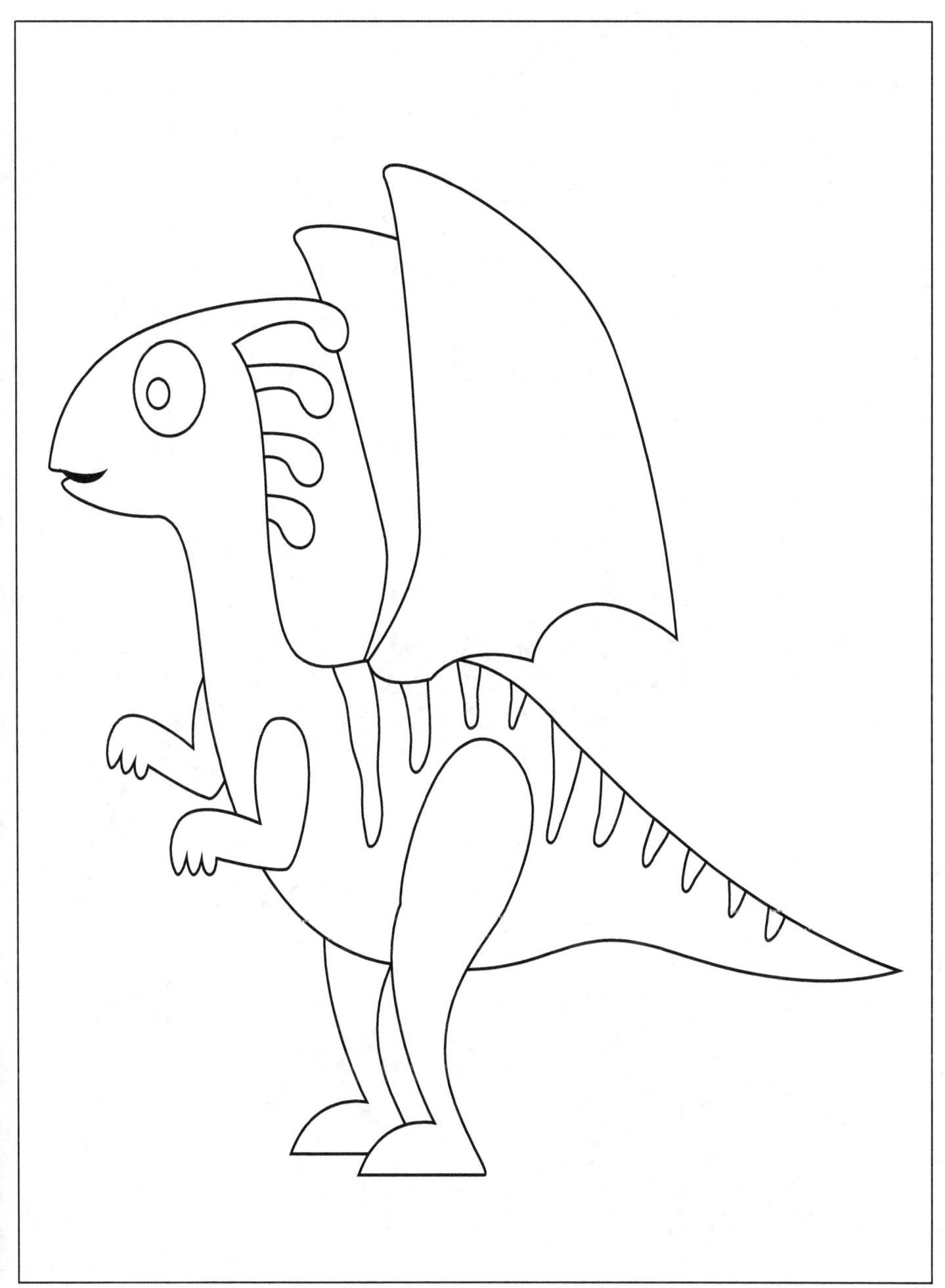

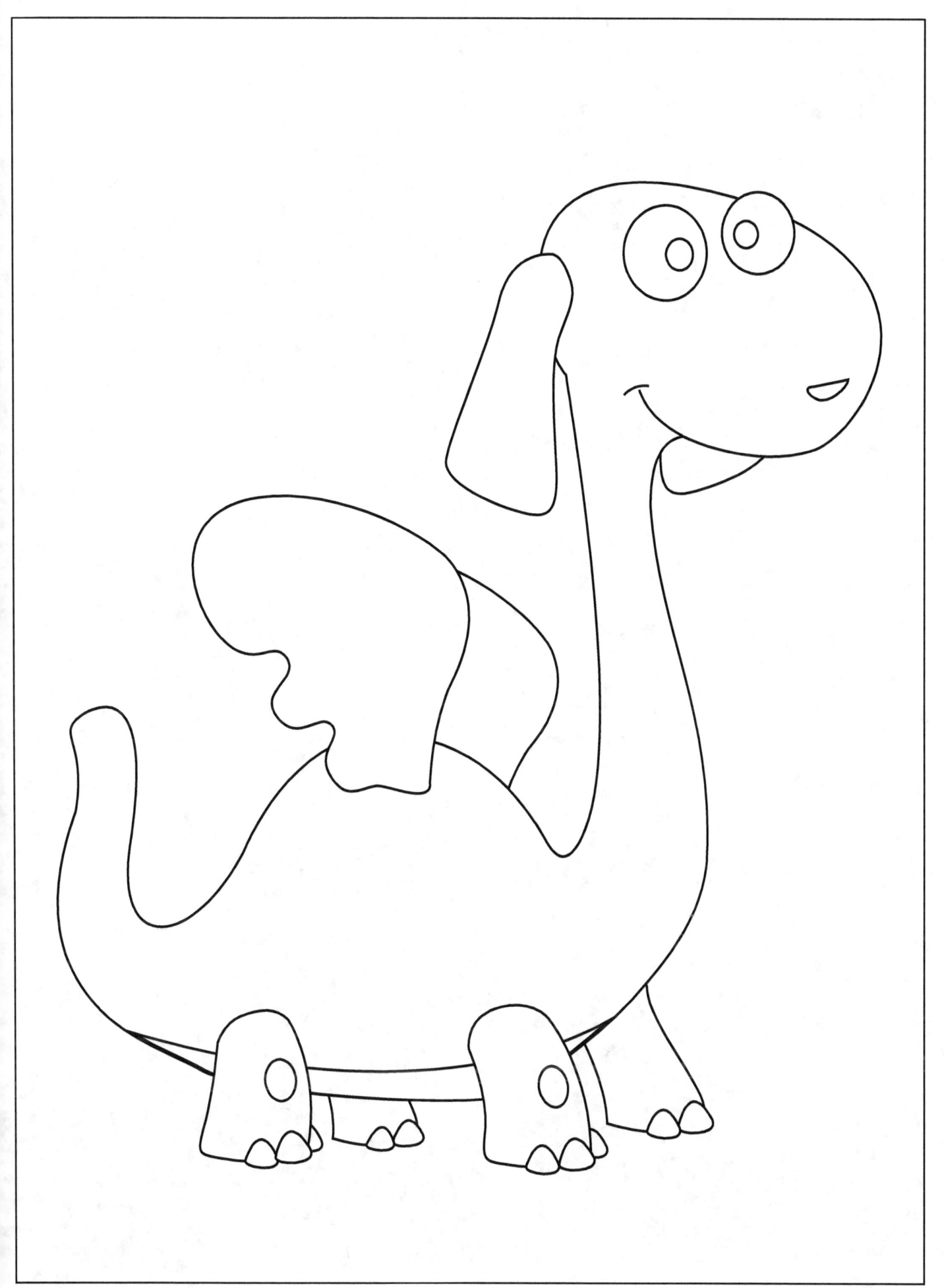

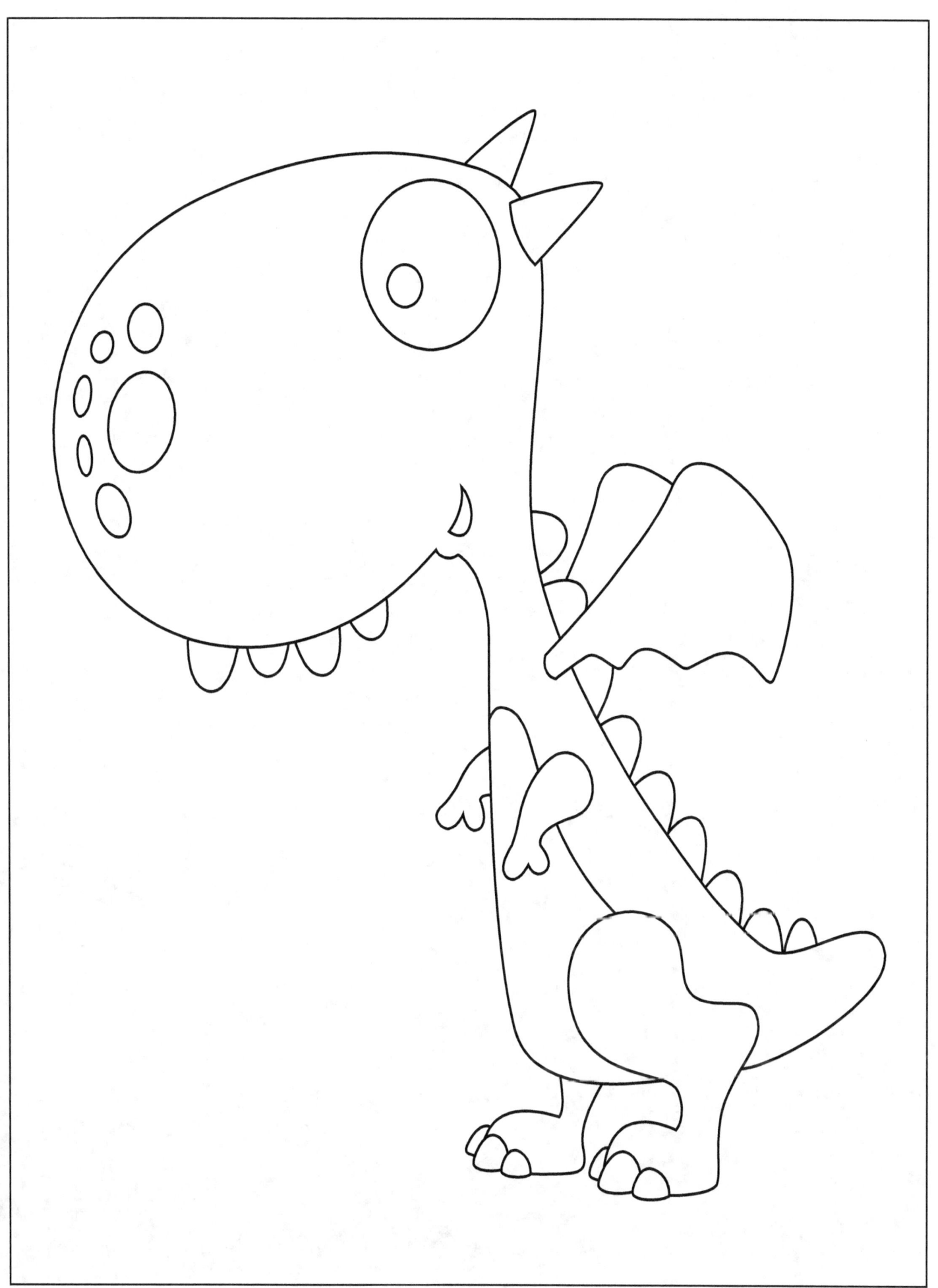

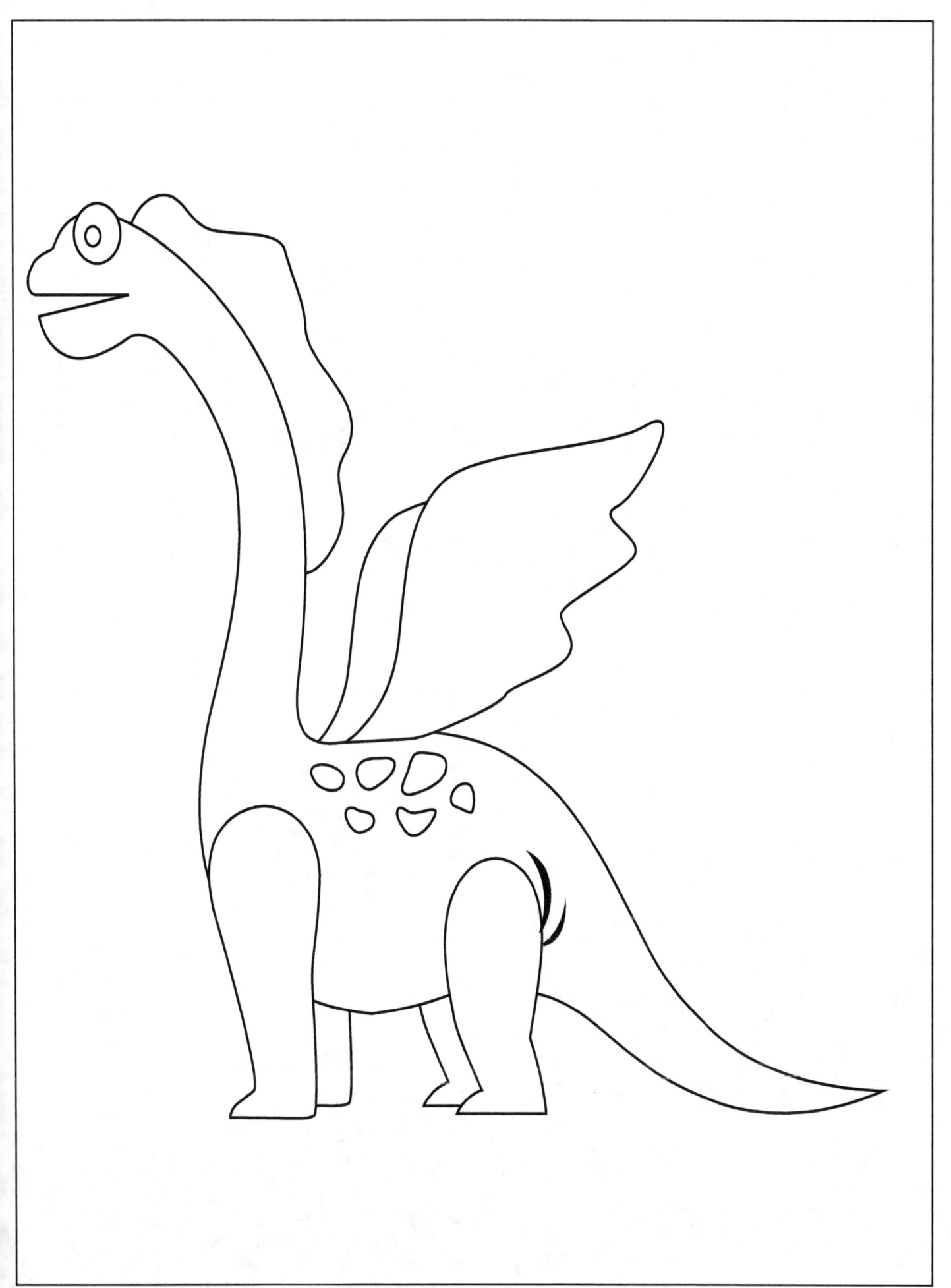

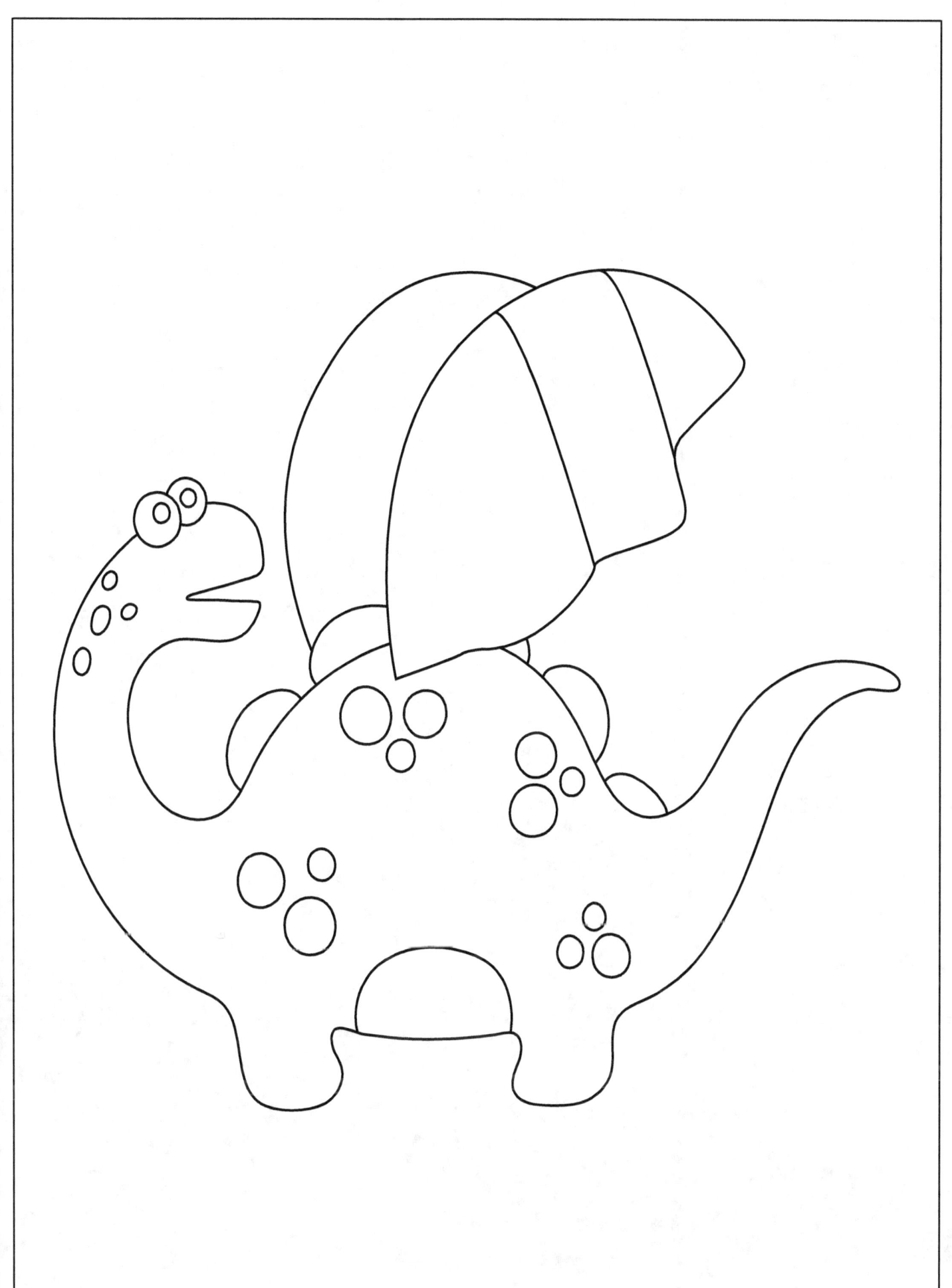

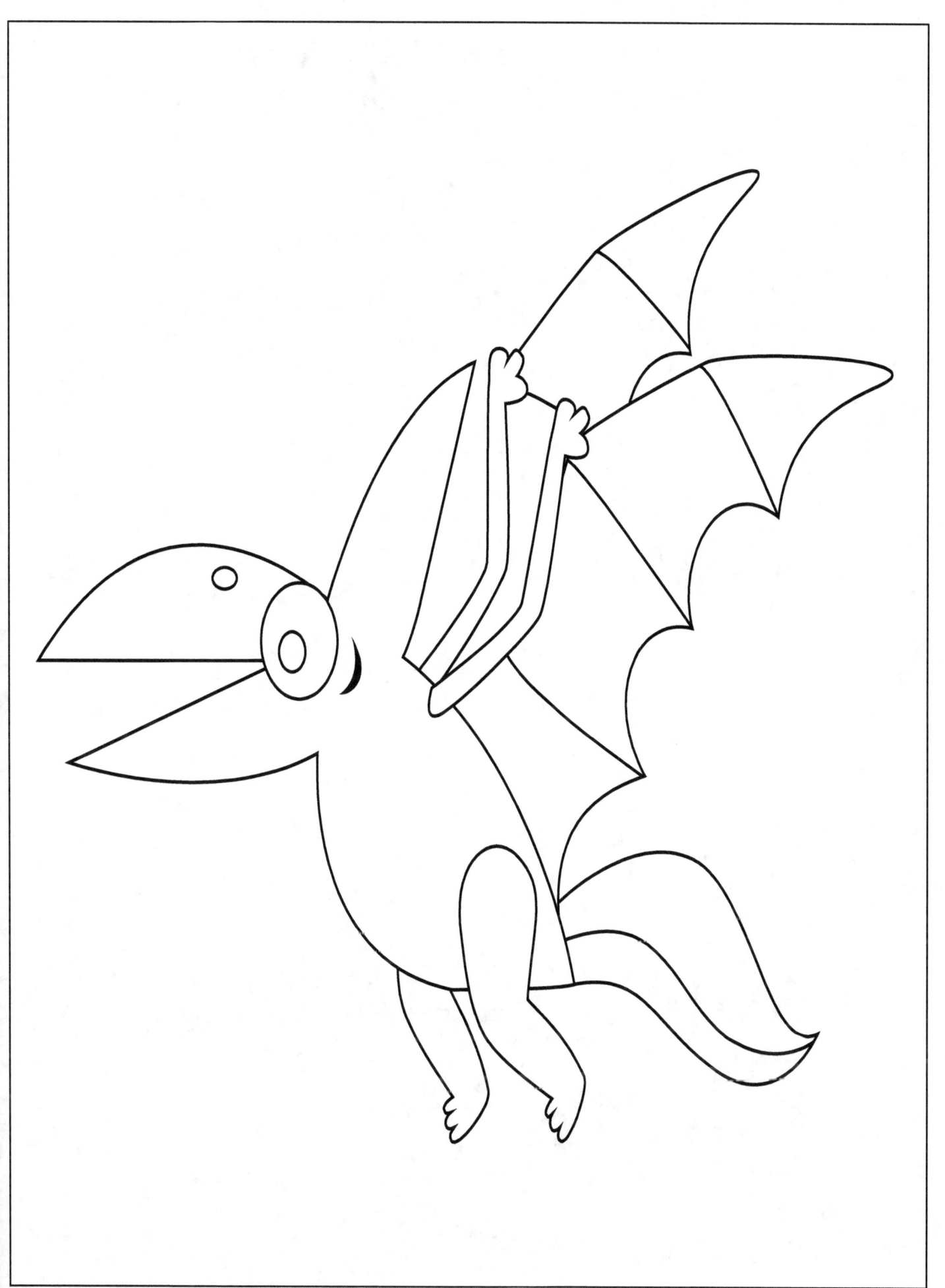

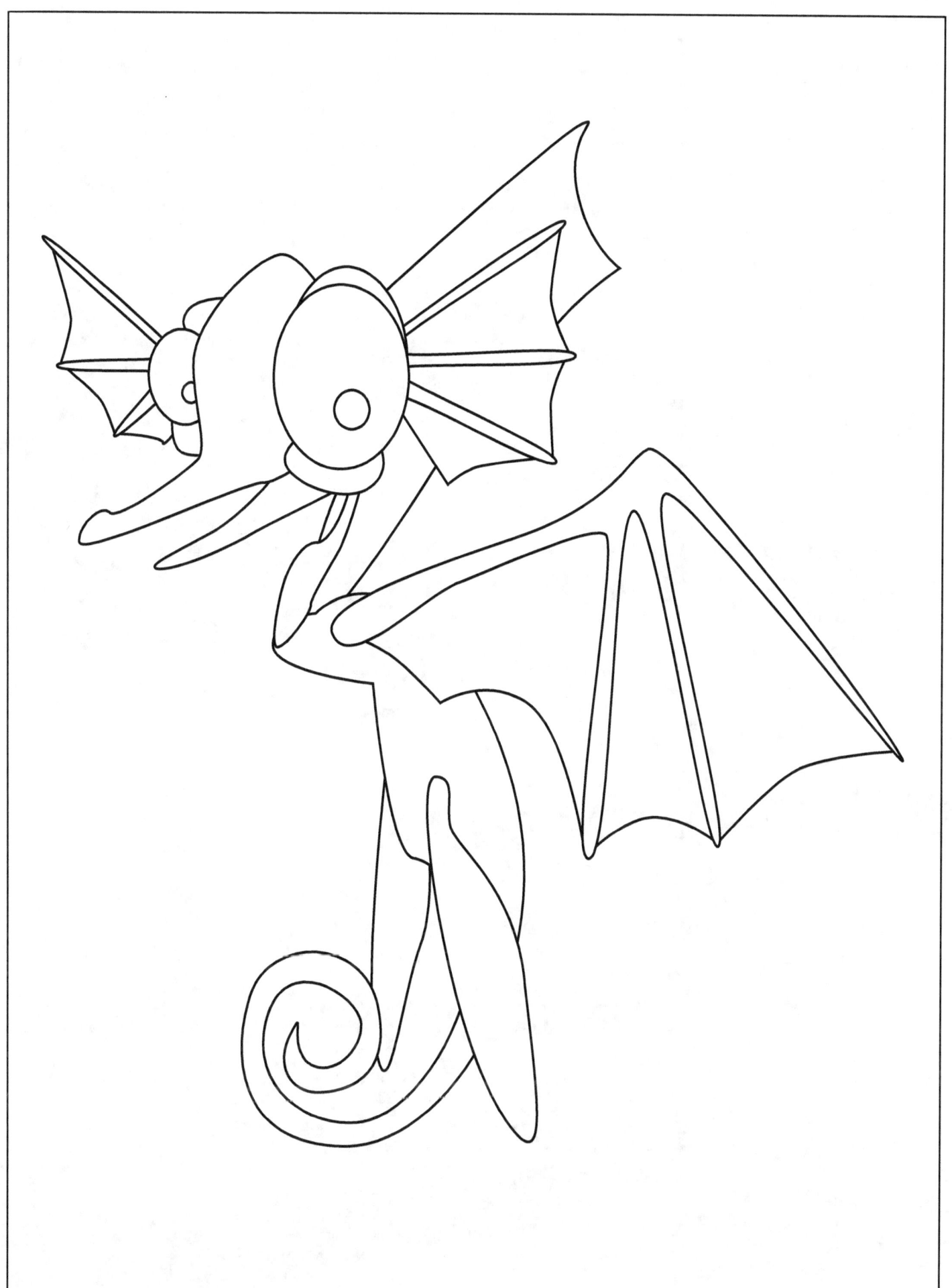

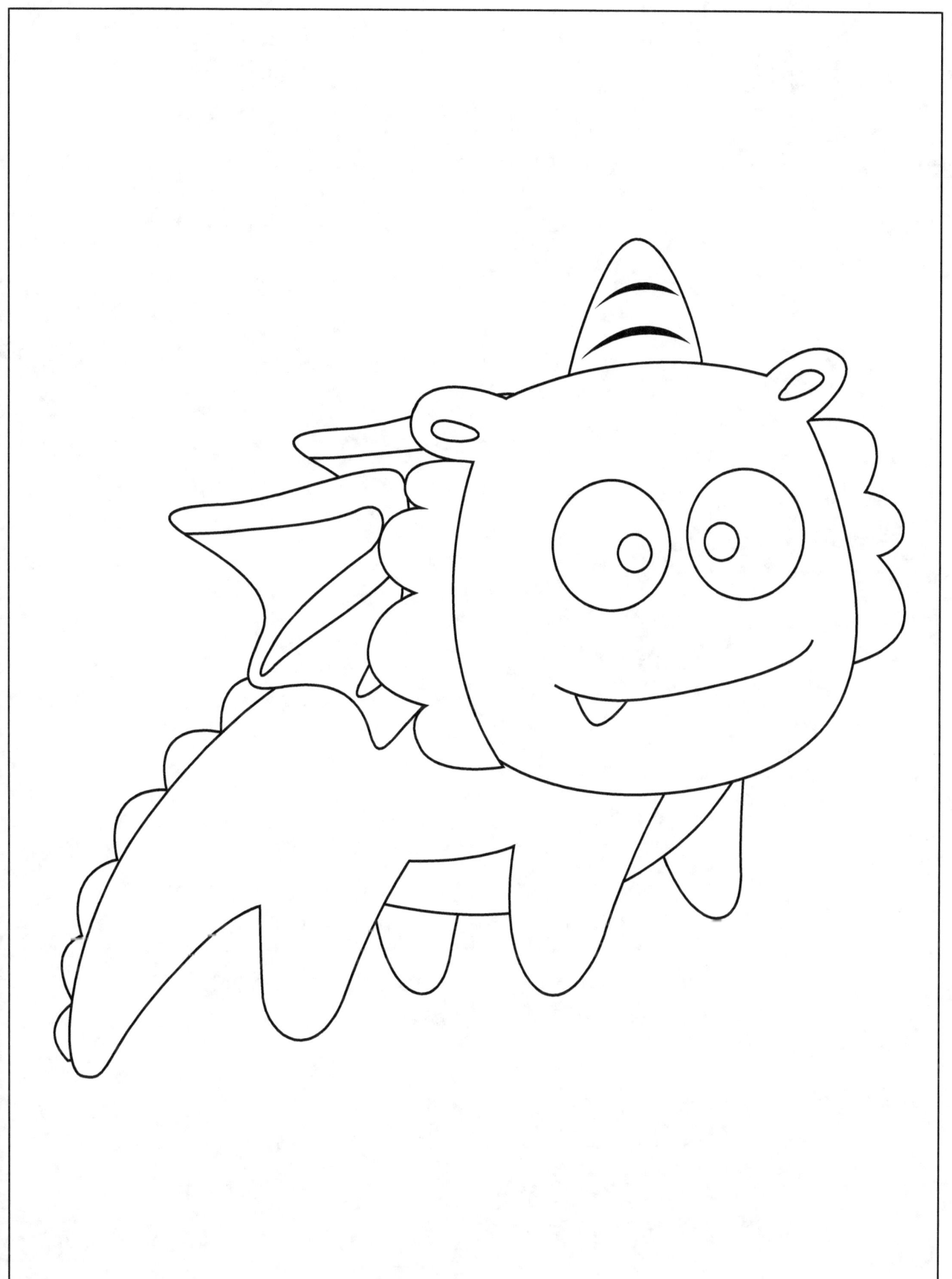

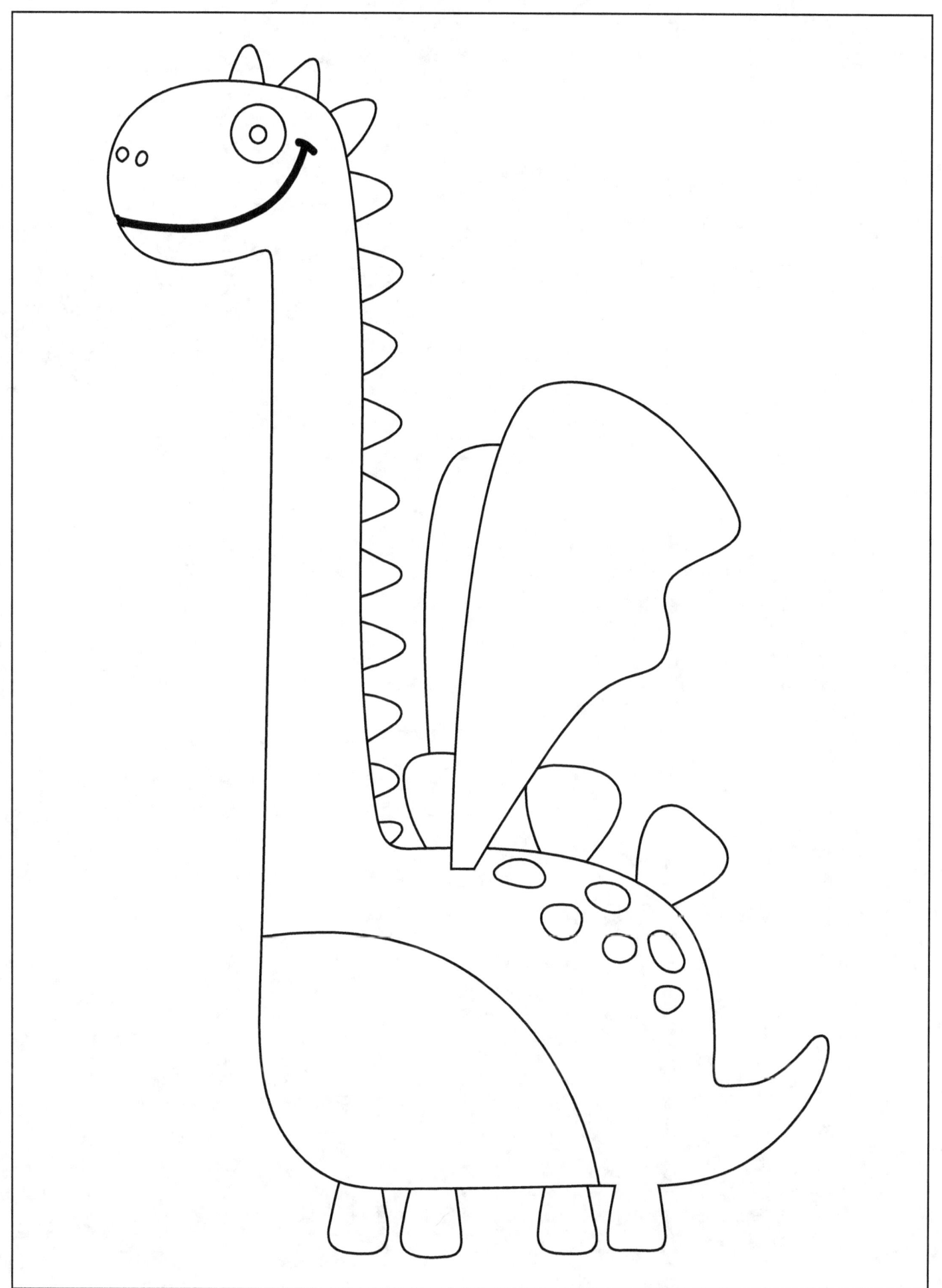

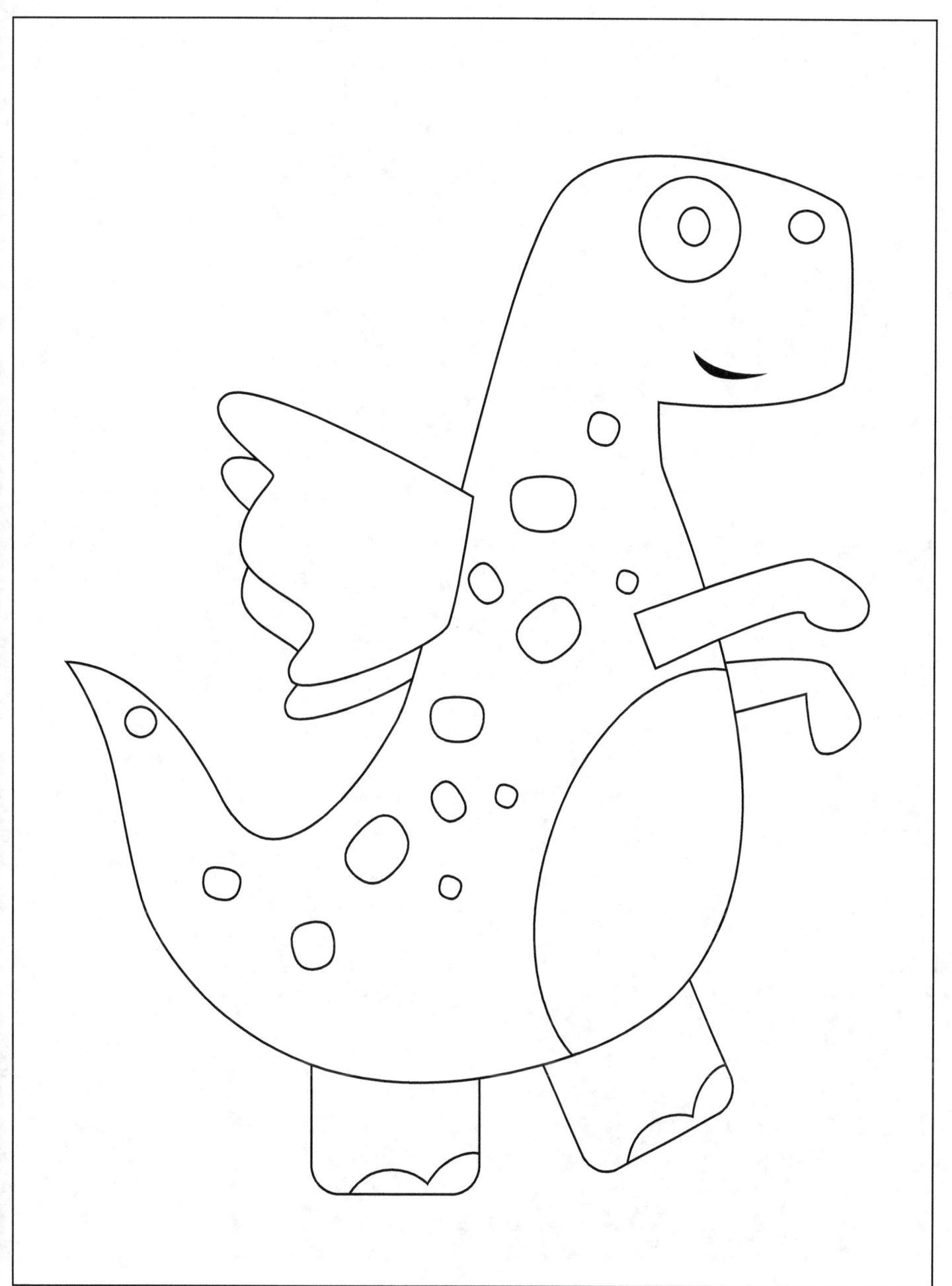

Source Images: Credit to - Danilo Sanino, IrynMerry, Chaika, Dukheva, VectorShow, NotionPic, Lanaart, Lo-kichen, Qvasimodo art, Zoo Hsiao, Marcio Nantes

www.ingramcontent.com/pod-product-compliance
Lightning Source LLC
Chambersburg PA
CBHW081736220526

45468CB00008B/2128